The Haitch Factor

ADVENTURES IN AUSTRALIAN ENGLISH

The Haitch Factor

ADVENTURES IN AUSTRALIAN ENGLISH

SUSAN BUTLER

MACMILLAN
Pan Macmillan Australia

First published 2014 in Macmillan by Pan Macmillan Australia Pty Ltd
1 Market Street, Sydney, New South Wales, Australia, 2000

Reprinted 2014

Cataloguing-in-Publication entry is available
from the National Library of Australia
http://catalogue.nla.gov.au

Typeset in 12/16.5 pt Adobe Garamond Pro by Midland Typesetters, Australia
Printed by McPherson's Printing Group

The author and the publisher have made every effort to contact copyright
holders for material used in this book. Any person or organisation that may have
been overlooked should contact the publisher.

Papers used by Pan Macmillan Australia Pty Ltd are natural, recyclable products
made from wood grown in sustainable forests. The manufacturing processes
conform to the environmental regulations of the country of origin.

To my most perceptive friend,
my husband Richard.

Table of Contents

Introduction

I like to joke that, as the editor of the *Macquarie Dictionary*, I am like the woman with the mop and bucket who comes along to clean up after the party is over. By this I mean that I do not create the mess. I am not devising the new words and bending the language to new uses. That is the consequence of the creative, not to say intoxicated, efforts of the language community. All I do is tidy up and decide what is worth putting in the dictionary and what goes out with the rubbish.

After a lifetime of such morning-after activity, I am in a good position to know what the successes and failures of the language have been. The usage notes in the dictionary are little reminders of such excitements, some of them generating broad discussion because this is the kind of party where both the fire brigade and the police have been called, the miscreants summoned before the court of pedants and censure meted out in all the word forums of the land. Others are of more academic interest causing the occasional chewing of the editorial blue pencil, or some educational angst about what should be promulgated in classrooms.

In all this the dictionary has tried to describe, as objectively as possible, what the language community seems to be doing and where it is headed. We have on occasion attempted to forge consensus with some of the major players in setting language style, but this is difficult. The very people who care passionately about language matters are the ones who are likely to be the most stubborn about particular issues.

As we make our language choices we should know when to care and when not to care. For myself, I care about 's plurals. This seems to me to be the one major blight on our texts at the moment and I wish something could be done about it. I would recommend losing the apostrophe completely rather than give in to the 's plurals.

In contrast to this, I think that, broadly speaking, variation should be accepted and that we should have greater tolerance of the choices made by others.

Watching the community arrive at these decisions and watching words take on histories and connotations that give them special significance in Australian English has shaped my days as editor. In that role I have to try to assess the mood of the language community.

But that still leaves me free to have personal likes and dislikes. This book is a mix of the objective view and the personal opinions developed over six editions of the dictionary. It covers a great range of topics, from usage matters to spelling, from origins of words to aspects of Australian English and of English around the world. As a dictionary editor I can't resist alphabetical order, so the items of discussion are linked by an intuitive sense of A to Z based on the words that I would give emphasis to in the headings.

I hope that readers find something of interest in this mix of observations and reflections. As for me, it is time to wield the mop and bucket again!

Aitch versus Haitch

Battle-weary though we all are, we must face up to the problem of *aitch* versus *haitch* yet again. Now I know that you have all instantly retreated to the trenches but come on out for a minute and consider the situation calmly.

For various historical reasons we have ended up with this variation in pronunciation. Those of you who say *aitch* would do well to bear in mind that an accident of linguistic change has meant that the Latin *ha* – the name for the letter that illustrated the aspiration – has been altered by degrees through *aha* to *ache* to *aitch*, a name that no longer illustrates aspiration.

The attempt to return the aspiration to the name is logical enough. Any child learning the alphabet understands that *a* is for 'apple' and *b* is for 'bat'. This is a good starting point for capturing the sound of letters, although already quite a lot has been glossed over in the creation of letter-to-sound equivalences. It is intuitively more logical to relate the name of the letter *h* to the aspirated rather than the unaspirated form. That is to say, *h* is for 'hat' rather than 'hour'. '*Haitch* is for "hat",' the child says. 'No! No! No!' we all yell. 'You must never, never say *haitch*. *Aitch* is for "hat".' It doesn't add up but the parental pain is evident so the children add it to the list of extraordinary and pointless things they are supposed to say and do while their parents are around.

Parents know that if their children pick their noses, neglect their teeth, say *haitch* instead of *aitch*, they will never make it in the world. It's as simple as that. *Haitch* is logical but not socially acceptable. Again history plays its part.

In Australia, the *haitch* pronunciation has been linked with Irish Catholics, the Marist Brothers in particular, although no real research has been done into this and it may well be hearsay or at best circumstantial. So the stigmatised pronunciation has been linked to a group who were traditionally the underdogs in Australian society.

It is remarkable that we fix on some idiosyncrasies of language as markers of the decline of Western civilisation, while others we are prepared to tolerate as acceptable variation. Of course, once such a pronouncement becomes entrenched in the language standards taught at school, the chances of the proscribed item ever being accepted are strongly diminished.

Why can't we regard this as a case of variant forms, as we do with 'schedule' (*skedjool* or *shedjool*) or 'harass' *(harass* or *huh'rass)*? Why does it create so much unnecessary heat? We ought to be able to dispassionately regard such strictures in our adult assessment of the relative importance of the bits of learning we acquired as part of our education.

Is it rather that we are reluctant to give up what seems so simple and obvious a proof of our own superiority?

People have fought wars because they felt superior to others. No one has done it yet on the basis of *haitch*, but it still remains an unnecessary social divider. You say *haitch*, I say *aitch*. Let's be tolerant of our little differences in language as in everything else.

In any case, the debate may roll over all of us because the young are endorsing *haitch* in ever-increasing numbers. Gender and social background no longer seem to have any bearing on the matter. It is in widespread use.

Feelings about alphabetical order

Most of us feel strongly about things at times. The war in Syria, the fate of the planet, who took the last biscuit when I wanted one for morning tea. But not many of us get worked up over alphabetical order. Not many of us realise, to begin with, that there is more than one kind of alphabetical order.

How to explain this without sending you to sleep? The following sequence of words is arranged in the manner that is the norm in the *Macquarie Dictionary*:

> *bush*
> *bushbaby*
> *bush-bash*
> *bush breakfast*
> *bushed*
> *bushwhacker*
> *bush wire*

This is a rigid style of ordering, where spaces and hyphens are ignored and you progress letter by letter.

Other dictionaries organise the presentation of the material differently, grouping all the words that are spaced or hyphenated under the first key item, so all the *bush* compounds of this kind might appear at *bush*, and the compounds that are set solid would have their own headword. The order in this system would be:

> *bush*
> *bush-bash*
> *bush breakfast*
> *bush wire*
> *bushbaby*
> *bushed*
> *bushwhacker*

There are arguments for and against, but *Macquarie*, like many other dictionaries, prefers the letter-by-letter arrangement. As we all know, English changes its mind about whether words are set solid, hyphenated or separated, so the letter-by-letter order avoids the change that would happen if we decided, for example, to spell *bushwhacker* as *bush whacker*.

Differences abound in this world and people can argue up a storm for various points of view. But we had one unusual caller who added a moral dimension to this. Her response to difference was to say that there is only one correct way. 'Why do you people take everything to the lowest common denominator?' she exclaimed with passionate feeling.

It seems that we attach connotations to everything we touch. Seeing difference leads us immediately to decisions about right and wrong, and inevitably to associations of love or hate. All on very little information.

Is it all right to be alright?

The process of change in language is not always smooth. The major bump is often a generational one, the older generation hanging on with increasing disbelief and outrage to what they know to be correct and the younger generation cruising on, so far from knowing that their usages are a departure from the norm that they are surprised, and then dismissive, when this is pointed out to them.

At *Macquarie* we have kept watch on the rising star of *alright* and have to announce that as of the fourth edition, it has equal place in the firmament with *all right*. Some of you will be shocked, I know. Some of you will mutter about *Macquarie*'s permissiveness. Instead of conducting public floggings of the miscreants, we meekly allow ourselves to be swayed by public and ignorant opinion. What can we do? Educated writers, published writers, writers from organisations with style guides and editors to police them have adopted *alright*. So be it. We are holding the line on *alot*, though. For now.

Our justification for this adjustment to the dictionary is that the language community seems to be equally divided over whether *alright* is acceptable or not. Of course what we expect to happen in due course is that this lexical item will follow the pattern of *already* and *altogether* where it is possible to distinguish between *already* meaning 'by this time' and *all ready* meaning 'all prepared'. Similarly we will be able to say 'The boys are alright' meaning 'they are comfortable, well, happy, etc.', and 'The boys are all right' meaning 'every single boy is correct in what he has done'. But at the moment we are still in a muddle, held back by the notion that *alright* is a shibboleth that educated people avoid.

Gazing at a crystal ball to predict the future of language changes like these is hazardous and unhelpful. So often it is the case that community opinion defies opposing forces, such as logic and the constant pressure of deviations, to maintain a perceived standard. Looking at student writing I would be prepared to bet that in another twenty years *alot* will be the norm. But even as I slapped my money on the table

I would experience a frisson of doubt. For how many centuries did the infinitive remain unrealistically and un-Englishly unsplit?

American English

Every year I look at the offerings from the American Dialect Society as an indicator of what new American English we might look forward to acquiring.

I can tell you that in the next few years, depending on the whims of the media, we may well acquire *binge-watch* (to consume vast quantities of a single show or series of visual entertainment in one sitting), or *hasher* (a fan of heavy metal music [origin unknown]), or *angst bunny* (a young woman with black clothes and lots of body piercing), or *glasshole* (a person made oblivious by wearing Google Glass, a head-mounted computer).

We talk of World English or International English, but these days to a large extent these names are synonymous with American English. Our English is not alone in being influenced in this way. Australian English, like British English, Singapore English and all the other varieties of English, is likely to pick up words like *cyberspace*, *push polling*, *spin doctor*, *wannabe* and *zine*. And on the whole these are very useful contributions and I'm not complaining.

So what does this say about Australian English? That we are heavily influenced by that other English? It's true. Mind you there has always been at least one pocket of the Australian community that has resisted this influence strenuously, but we are constantly undone by the children who seem to have no shame when it comes to clamouring for *take-out* rather than *take-away*, referring to *blokes* as *dudes* and everyone as *guys*, and regarding those who don't use this language as *dorks* or *dweebs*.

And the other traitors in our ranks are the journalists who mop up new words like inky sponges and then leak them all over our newspapers. A *couch potato* was a term invented as a joke on *boob tuber*, someone who sits in front of the boob tube. This one was picked up by *The New Yorker* magazine in mid-1987 but took only six months to make it into the pages of *The Sun News-Pictorial* in Australia.

But are we swamped completely?

I can also look through commentaries on American English and find that the following items, though current in American English, seemed to have no particular charm for us: *ear candy* (popular music that is not strident or loud), *funsome* (full of fun or very funny), *cocktail farm* (a neat and tidy farm not run as a working business) and *white-collar overalls* (a business suit). We are choosey about what we take from American English although sometimes it doesn't seem that way. And to counter the American intake we do have the ballast of what is already established in the lexicon of Australian English.

Recently our anxiety has stemmed from the perception that our national variety of English is losing its distinctive lexicon, and that the next generation of Australian children have no interest in lexical Australiana. There is no sign of *fair dinkum* or *bewdy*, I will admit, except in tones of heavy irony. On the other hand I do find *bludger, boofhead, dodgy, dropkick, dunny* and *purler* reinvented as *pearler*.

Children always want a new style, in language as in clothes, to differentiate themselves from the oldies and, conversely, to identify themselves as being one of their generation. But it seems to me that they have not entirely abandoned the past.

Nor should change be seen as threatening our variety of English. We mustn't confuse culture with language, and imagine that to remain Australians we must straightjacket ourselves in the vocabulary of yesteryear.

Nor should we imagine that every change we see is another example of the invasion of American English.

I remember a caller who was very upset about a supposed Americanised spelling. To my astonishment the word that was causing grief turned out to be *dispatch*. The caller, somewhat coldly, wanted to ask whether the correct spelling was *dispatch* or *despatch*. I replied that we gave *dispatch* as the headword but listed *despatch* as a legitimate variant. This was not good enough. My caller suddenly spilled the beans, although still somewhat aggrievedly. His teacher in primary school had insisted that *despatch* was the correct spelling and woe betide them if they produced *dispatch*. In a spelling bee, it would win no points. Was this yet another example of American spelling overtaking traditional Australian spelling? He and his friends had been comparing notes over morning tea and he had decided to get to the bottom of it all.

Almost any problem in Australian spelling or usage is sheeted home to pernicious American influence and often the *Macquarie Dictionary* is accused of aiding and abetting this crumbling of our culture and standards, because it is seen simultaneously as an attack on Aussie culture and a lapse in standards away from the prestige British form. In this case I was able to explain that the form *despatch* had crept into English as a headword in Dr Samuel Johnson's dictionary. Since he himself used the *dispatch* spelling and since all the citations he had were for *dispatch*, the theory is that it was a typographical error. Ever since, English spelling has wavered and not been entirely sure whether to *dispatch* or *despatch*. My caller had the grace to laugh and to promise that he would report all this back to his friends. It was all very interesting, we agreed.

How particular and severe we can be on matters that cause no concern to others. How readily we give way to our feelings about odd aspects of language without checking the facts. And how surprisingly strong those feelings are!

The proliferating apostrophe

I suppose the most surprising thing about the apostrophe is not that it has suddenly started causing us problems, but that we have been able to hold the line for so long. The apostrophe is essentially an artifice of writing, a grammarian's flourish imposed from above rather than a popular creation arising from real need.

Old English was inflected and had a possessive case, so it was possible to indicate that the king *owned* the castle by using the possessive form of *king*, which was *kinges* (pronounced as two syllables) – the *kinges castle*. By a process of elision, in which one spoken syllable slides into another, the disyllabic *kinges* became the monosyllabic *kings*. Grammarians of the 17th century – the same ones who gave us endless hang-ups about the split infinitive – decided that that the elided syllable should be indicated and introduced the apostrophe to mark its absence.

It is true that the apostrophe is used legitimately in this fashion even now – we introduce it when we are conscious that something has been left out. For example, *'cos* for 'because' and *o'er* for 'over'.

The problem arose with the contrastive pair – *its* and *it's*. The first is the possessive form of *it* – handed down to us all the way from Old English. The second is the elided form of *it is*. School children and learners of English grasp the fact that apostrophe *s* marks the possessive but then have to deal with this exceptional pair where the one without the apostrophe is the possessive.

For generations we have managed to inculcate this grammatical lesson into the children well enough for it to be maintained more or less in the general run of adult texts. Whether it is the faltering of the grammatical tradition in our schools or the influx of a migrant community for whom English is a second language that has caused the current difficulty, who can say? The worst aspect of this malaise is that the apostrophe is often added, in a fit of panic, before the final -*s* that marks the plural form. So we have *two dog's* and *three cat's*, *four house's* and *five vehicle's*.

And from there the disease has spread to pronouns – *your* and *you're* have been irretrievably confused, and *yours* has become *you'rs*.

The problem is not just an Australian one – it is current in Britain as well, where the misplaced apostrophe has been labelled *the greengrocer's apostrophe* from its frequent appearance on fruit shop signs (*tomato's*, *avo's*, etc.).

There is some speculation that nouns ending in *-o* are badly affected because the anxiety about the apostrophe is made worse by the anxiety about the plural form: 'Does it have an *-es* or just an *-s*?' The following is from an ad that appeared in the *Sun-Herald* on 3 March 1996: 'Ever wondered what 5 Kilo's of fat looks like?' There is also the amusing ambiguity of the ad for 'Coco's palms' – the 'palms of Mr Coco' or the 'palms from Cocos Island'?

Apostrophes in place names are a particular difficulty. A council in Devon has banned the apostrophe from all road signs, causing uproar among the defenders of English punctuation. The US has advocated abandoning the apostrophe in place names since the 1890s, and the Australian Geographical Names Board did likewise in 1966, so that we have Kings Cross, not King's Cross, for example.

It is possible to defend the apostrophe in ordinary text while allowing that once the type size gets over a certain point, we read it slightly differently. The design element seems to outweigh other considerations. Kings Cross in very big type looks neat, while King's Cross looks untidy. In the context of signage, we have a limited set of forms that can be identified quite easily, so that the chances for ambiguity are few. You could argue that we don't need punctuation on a street sign in the way that we need it in text.

It would be a far, far better thing if we were to forgo the apostrophe entirely, expunge it from our writing completely rather than let it loose to rampage amongst our plurals. It never did much harm or good, although it certainly gave us something to think about at school. We could manage perfectly well relying on context alone. The *kings castle* is just as clearly meaningful as the *king's castle*. We do this already with expressions of time, as in *in three months time, in four days time*. So I would be prepared to lead a 'Down with the Apostrophe' campaign rather than suffer in silence while they multiply like rabbits and warren our writing to the point where the reader cannot negotiate any text safely without falling down an apostrophe hole.

Disappearing Australianisms

On Australia Day 2007, the *Macquarie Dictionary* launched a small survey from its website of what might be thought of as some traditional Australiana in Australian English, just to test the waters. The list comprised items that I thought would obviously have gone out of favour (*the traps* for 'the police', *cove* for 'a person'), others that I thought were borderline and doubtful (*shickered* for 'drunk', *troppo*, *bonzer*, *beyond the black stump*) and others that I thought might surprise us (*fair dinkum*, *furphy*, *lurk*). In the end, this impressionistic survey seemed to show that, as we suspected, the bush is clinging to traditional Australian English whereas the city is shedding it. There was general support from the bush in the middle age group (18–25) for Australiana such as *cocky*, *billabong*, *the mallee*, *fossick*, *bludger*, *wowser*, *beyond the black stump*, *lurk*, *brass razoo*, *cobber*, *battler*, *troppo* and *galah*, all of which received less support from the same age group in the city.

Items that were definitely out were *shickered*, *cobber* and *sleep-out* and items that were really doubtful were *new chum* and *spinebashing*. There did seem to be a surprising amount of support for *fair dinkum*, *bonzer*, *furphy* and *wowser*, although it has to be said that in the comparison between those under 17 and those over 60 (where differences were much sharper) the under-17s denied all knowledge of *furphy* and gave very limited support to *wowser*. I had expected them to turn their backs on *fair dinkum* as well, but it was not so. Still, this was a very broad and unsubtle survey and did not allow them to register ironic use.

I expect the pattern to be still very much the same. There has been a turn in the cultural tide that makes some of the established items of Australian English seem very dated now. Fashion in language may well revive some of them. I have noticed that *purler* has been resurrected in the language of the younger generation but is now re-invented, etymologically speaking, as *pearler*. That is to say, it is linked to the pearl of great price rather than the British dialect word *to purl* (to move along smoothly and easily) from which it follows that a *purler* is something excellent. Leaving aside the spelling and the confusion, it is nice to know that the word is still with us.

None of these words will disappear from the dictionary but they may well acquire the label *Dated* and, if they continue to fall out of favour, ultimately the label *Obsolete*. There is a common expectation that, as we load in words like *technomite* and *yarn bombing* and *tmoz*, we will be shovelling out words like the above. Not so, because these are precisely the sorts of words that people will need to look up if they are reading the literature of previous centuries, for example. The dictionary in print may have finite borders but fortunately the dictionary online can cope with it all.

Australian values

From time to time there is much talk about Australian values and the necessity for newcomers to the country to understand concepts like 'fair dinkum'. But perhaps there are some other words that might be considered as part of the essential lexicon of Australian values. What about 'dobbing', for example. Should all applicants for a citizenship demonstrate their ability to dob to the satisfaction of a review committee, and should the applicant know that whereas dobbing was once a bad thing, it is now considered a virtuous activity? My local council recently invited residents to 'dob in a dumper' and presumably the citizens took up this great Australian invitation with pride.

Professor Anna Wierzbicka of the Australian National University lists *dob*, along with a number of other negatives such as *whingeing* and *wowserism*, as key words of Australian culture. Why such negativity? Well, it seems that these are the values that we pass on to our children by telling them what NOT to do. There seems to be a grain of truth in that. I'm sure that parents are still telling their children to stop whingeing. As the children get older, they tell each other not to be such a wanker. In Australia, our aspirations are to avoid the mud rather than seek the stars.

The positives are harder to enshrine in language. No self-respecting child today would use the expression *fair dinkum*, although they know these 'old Australian' words and expressions and can call on them for self-conscious effect. This generation is all too postmodernist and mocking and relative about everything to feel comfortable wearing unsophisticated approbation on their sleeve.

I have noticed the way in which the boys use the word *mate*. More like 'maaaa ayte'! As I listened and observed, I realised this was a swift send-up of what they think of as old-fashioned blokey behaviour, of traditional Australian male ways expressing traditional Australian values.

Sometimes 'maaaa ayte' is accompanied by 'ba luddy ba yewdy' in an extended version, indicating that the great Australian adjective is also an object of scorn. Any serious anger or delight is these days addressed by the 'f-word'.

So are we handing on traditional values or are we just sending ourselves up? And is that in itself the traditional Australian way of not taking anything too seriously for fear that enthusiasm might bite us and we might become that Australian no-no, the ratbag? It may be a peculiarly Australian difficulty to track culture in language, when the constant thrust of the culture is to subvert the language.

Authorise or authorize?

A school in Queensland caused a stir by using the spelling *authorization* with a z on its public noticeboard.

This sparked a debate on radio as to what the correct spelling should be and *Macquarie Dictionary* was asked to adjudicate.

The problem is an etymological one. Words that derive from Ancient Greek via Latin take the *-ize* ending to show their link to the Greek ending *-izein*. Words that have come into English from Old French take *-ise* to reflect the French ending.

This would be wonderful if we all knew our Greek and Latin and Old French and had the time to consider etymologies as we employed our words. In the absence of that knowledge, we seek a practical solution.

If you use the *-ise* spelling you have one exception – *capsize* – which cannot, for etymological reasons, take the *-ise* ending because, curiously, the origin of *capsize* is unknown. It has nothing to do with this debate.

If you go the other way and adopt the *-ize* ending, there is a larger list of exceptions, words that do not go back to Latin and Greek. Words like *advertise*, *advise*, *comprise, compromise, despise, devise, exercise, improvise, revise, surprise, televise.*

Of course you can disregard etymology completely and decide to spell everything with *-ise* or, alternatively, everything with *-ize*, and this is happening. The British think of the Americans as having adopted the *-ize* spelling for everything, while the Americans comment that the British way of doing business is to use *-ise*. Back in the first edition of the *Style Manual*, published in 1966 by the Commonwealth Government Printing Office, the decision was made that the Australian way would be to use *-ise* because we thought that was British. Of course the real picture is much more confused.

Authorise is an interesting case because it does go back to Latin and Greek and therefore, etymologically speaking, should have *-ize*. The general style guide has overridden this and usually in Australian English, it is spelled *authorise*. But there is always the exception.

Nathan Bailey – my favourite lexicographer

Take any page of Nathan Bailey's *Universal Etymological English Dictionary* and you learn fascinating snippets of information about England in the early 1700s.

Take Bailey's view of politics. In his dictionary, the words *democracy* and *republic* are lacking, *king* is minimally defined and *parliament* a little more warmly described. The astonishing entries are those for *knight* and *gentleman*, which are both very lengthy and list the rights of those who had achieved such status.

For example, 'The evidence of a gentleman was accounted more authentic than that of a peasant' and 'A gentleman condemned to death was not to be hanged but beheaded; nor was his examination to be taken with torture'. Bailey ends with the sad comment, 'In our days all are accounted gentlemen, that have money, and if he has no coat of arms, the king of arms can sell him one'.

His disillusionment is also evident at the entry for *knight* in which he observes that knights were supposed to be good and brave and daring and undaunted and the ceremony at which a knight was created was a serious affair, 'but now the honour being grown cheap, these ceremonies have been laid aside, and there goes nothing now to the making of a knight in England but the King's touching with a sword as he kneels and saying "Rise up Sir R.N. [Right Name]".'

Dictionaries reveal the enthusiasms of their authors, in this case towards classical learning. Bailey justifies this in his preface by pointing out that 'it is so common among our modern poets to intersperse the Grecian and Roman theology, mythology, etc. in their works, an unacquaintance with which renders their writings either obscure or at least less intelligible to the readers', that he felt compelled to bung them all in.

An example of this sort of thing is the long entry at *sacrifice*, which reads like a cross between a recipe book and a book of etiquette.

After the introduction, Bailey provides the detail of how to do your own sacrifice. First take your sacrificial beast. Then mix a small quantity of salt and meal. Then taste the wine. Pour the rest between the horns of the beast and pulling a few hairs from the place, throw them into the fire. Then slay the beast by knocking him down or cutting his throat. Then with a long knife, turn the bowels up and down. Under no circumstances touch with the hands. I won't go on but Bailey did. *Burning the dead* is a good entry too.

The entry for *rain*, in which Bailey provides all the current theories about its causes, is an opportunity for him to display his knowledge of the cutting-edge science of his day.

His definition of *hail* is a 'meteor formed of flocks of snow, which is melted and then refrozen into smaller stones'. And *snow* is a thick cloud 'reduced into the form of carded wool. The white colour of snow proceeds from the conjunction of humidity with cold which naturally engineers whiteness'.

Dr Johnson relied heavily on Bailey's dictionary in the compilation of his own, but his interests were literary rather than scientific so his entry for *rain* reads: 'The moisture that falls from the clouds'. He then gives three literary citations and adds a note to the effect that:

Rain is water by the heat of the sun divided into very small parts ascending into the air, 'til encountering the cold, it be condensed into clouds, and descends in drops.

True, true. But where is the passion? Where is the search for the detail of how it is done?

The language captured in the dictionary reflects the dominant culture of the day. Often it helps to be at some remove to be able to see it more clearly. Dictionaries that are close up and contemporary will inevitably be so much in accord with our world view that, if they are any good, we find them unremarkable.

Will we in 100 years, 200, 300, have the same sense of history as we pick up today's *Macquarie Dictionary*? Will the book that we use on a day-to-day basis because we can't remember how many 'm's there are in 'committee', reveal at a future date its other function – to be a record of our culture, caught up in the lexicon of our time and in the meanings that we give the words that we choose to use?

Already I find that the Word of the Year pages collected on the *Macquarie* website provide that backwards look to a different world. In 2006 the chosen word was *muffin top*. The next year we had *pod slurping* and *password fatigue*. The year after that the GFC had struck and the word of the year was *toxic debt*. We can be reminded on a year-by-year basis of what the events were that governed our lives as they are reflected in the words we use.

Bandicoot

The bandicoot was initially regarded as one of the many strange new creatures encountered in Australia and joined such animals as the kangaroo, koala, emu and wombat as stereotypical wildlife. The bandicoot was regarded as a pest by farmers and gardeners because of its habit of digging for grubs and roots. It was also regarded as sport for hunting and as good eating. And it was noted that the bandicoot was easily tamed and could become a household pet.

Expressions that grew up about the bandicoot are based on its lean appearance. It was described as 'poor' and 'miserable', that is, in a wretched condition. Just to increase the pathos, the phrase *miserable as a bandicoot* was expanded to *miserable as a bandicoot on a burnt ridge*, the idea being that a bushfire had deprived the bandicoot of home and sustenance. It was also noted that the bandicoot carried ticks – thus the play on lousy meaning both 'infested with lice' and 'mean'. If the land was dry and had little fodder, then the last animal to be able to survive was thought to be the bandicoot. Any land that was so bad that it couldn't support a bandicoot was in a very bad way indeed. And so the bandicoot became a symbol of privation and wretchedness.

Later phrases are probably extensions of the basic meaning of isolated and wretched and are prompted by alliteration, as in *barmy as a bandicoot*.

In the 1800s a makeshift dwelling, usually just some supports with strips of bark over them, was called a *bandicoot gunyah*.

In the early 1900s the bandicoot was romanticised by writers along with other Australian wildlife. It does seem to have been regarded in all personifications as slightly stupid and of low status, and as having a blend of timidity and cunning. The bandicoot in *The Magic Pudding* captures all these qualities.

The verb *to bandicoot* derives from potato farming in Victoria in the 1890s. It captures the action of digging around the roots of the potato plant to steal the tubers without disturbing the plant.

The little word *because*

The word *because* has for many years been described as a conjunction. *I know that it is daytime because the sun is up.*

It was slightly complicated by turning up in a prepositional phrase *because of. We can go on holidays because of your generosity.*

But it is being used in a different way now.

Why are you sad? Because reasons. Because because.

What follows *because* can be pretty well anything and so the construction is being described as *because* x.

Why are you happy? Because yay.

Why are you cross? Because need. Because want.

The construction is colloquial, involving as it does a shorthand that will be understood by the speaker and the listener sharing a context and knowing that, as friends, they can reduce a whole clause to a single word as a kind of amiable shorthand. It's friendly and cool.

The pronunciation of *Beijing*

The pronunciation of foreign names is always a matter of delicate balance. It is hard for most of us to fight our way past our own speech patterns established within our own variety of English to sounds and combinations that exist in other languages. There has always been a tendency for people in specialised fields to care more about this than the rest of us – the ongoing debate about the correct pronunciation of *Don Juan* is sometimes more clearly seen as a conflict between the music community who take their pronunciation from a foreign language (say *don wan*) and the general community who have inherited a well-established pronunciation in English (say *don jewan*). In recent times, however, there has been a widely held feeling in the community that good manners obliges us to make the attempt to pronounce someone's name as that person would pronounce it, and to produce the names of cities in a fashion that at least approximates the pronunciation that the citizens of those cities would offer, unless there is a very well-established English pronunciation, as is the case with Paris, or indeed another spelling – *München* vs *Munich*.

The pronunciation of *Beijing* would, in Chinese, have a hard *jing* as in *jingle*. The fact that many of us feel that we must soften the *jing* is perhaps another example of what has been described as the Universal French Accent, which Australians commonly apply to any foreign word. French was the foreign language that most older Australians today would have encountered at school and French pronunciation patterns were the most generally understood of all foreign languages, in particular the nasalised *an*, which Australians apply to words ending in *-in*, *-en*, *-an*, or *-ain* indiscriminately. *Bonjour* is a familiar word, and we know that the *j* there is soft. So confronted with a foreign word, *Beijing*, we instinctively soften the *j* in that as well. But in Chinese this is a mistake. It is a case of learning a few rules about how one foreign language behaves and generalising wildly. With the best of intentions, of course.

The Bible

Two great texts have had profound influence on the English language – the works of Shakespeare and the King James version of the Bible. Both have left such traces as items of vocabulary, but more importantly as idioms, as stereotypes, as stories that we all share.

Many of the lexical items that we would instantly associate with those texts are archaisms – words preserved in the aspic of great writing, and protected from the kind of changes that are wrought from day to day on lesser language. Brows beetle, the rump fed ronyon is aroined.

There are others that have generalised from their particular meaning to a wider use and that we think of as contemporary English. Outside the Bible we can experience an epiphany when we have any kind of deep insight, we can be drawn into an apocalypse when we experience a great disaster.

These texts have contributed to our language in other ways. Our world is peopled by Judases or Shylocks, we have the patience of Job or the ardour of Romeo and we applaud those who are good Samaritans. We complain when something is a mill-stone around our necks. We know that pride goes before a fall (a very abbreviated version of a Proverb) and we should neither a borrower nor a lender be (from the speech of Polonius).

The stories themselves are there as reference and illustration. Romeo and Juliet, the Tower of Babel, Cain and Abel – these can all serve as parallels to a contemporary experience.

But to what extent do we still draw on these resources? Once the Bible and Shakespeare were frequently quoted, although there is a theory that Samuel Butler's *Hudibras* would rate higher than either of them. The Bible may well have been quoted as much for ecclesiastical point-scoring as for the embel-lishment of writing but both works provided common ground between the writer and the reader, the speaker and the listener. Nowadays this is no longer true.

The common ground for contemporary reference is more likely to be popular culture – the movies and TV shows that achieve the kind of popularity that means that a shared understanding is possible. *Seinfeld* is an excellent source of quotes such as 'Yadda, yadda, yadda', or 'Not that there's anything wrong with that!'

The 'soup Nazi' lives on and has turned into the 'nipple-Nazi'. *Sesame Street* provides snippets of wisdom ('It's not easy being green') that our community will acknowledge.

'The writing's on the wall' is a remark that people today would certainly understand – they would take it to mean that a negative outcome is a certainty. But as they use this phrase they would not have in mind its origin – the grim moment in Belshazzar's feast, recounted in the Book of Daniel, when the moving finger wrote a message of imminent doom on the wall. For those of you who don't know the ending, Belshazzar, King of Babylon, whose crime was having profaned the sacred vessels taken from the Temple in Jerusalem, was killed that night by the Persians.

On the one hand there is no reason to complain. As long as we all share our understanding of the phrase it doesn't matter what its origin was. But somehow, with referential idioms like this, it does seem that we lose something when they are cut adrift from the story and the image that gave rise to them.

It is scarcely possible to quote Shakespeare today except in jest. 'My kingdom for a horse' you might say when you have just missed the bus. The family has a pet frog called Yorick whose passing allows them to say

'Alas, poor Yorick …'. The Bible would be even harder to work into the average conversation. Do we regretfully say goodbye to the familiar idioms these writings produced and is there now a cultural divide between those whose mental wallpaper is classical and those for whom it is entirely contemporary?

The mystery of the bogan

No one is quite sure of the origin of *bogan* although there is general agreement that it is a word that became current in the 1980s. We have various places — some real and some imaginary — that are linked with stereotypes in expressions in Australian English, for example, *back of Bourke*, or *Hell and Hay and Booligal*, or *Bullama-kanka*, or *Woop Woop*. *Bogan* appears in the phrase *a bogan shower*, which, with typical outback irony, is a dust storm. Then we have the *bogan gate*, which is something improvised out of some barbed wire and a few droppers. So *bogan* becomes associated with the rough-and-ready makeshift ways of the bush. It is the opposite of city sophistication.

So someone who is rough and ready and unsophis-ticated is a bogan. There is a general notion of how this stereotype dresses (flannos and ugg boots and mullet hairdos) and eats (pizza and Coke).

Other theories are that *bogan* derives from the name of a person. This is a standard way of arriving at words for stereotypes. In Queensland the *bogan* is a *bevan* (from the name Bevan). Other examples are *Bazza* for a brash Australian male, *Kimmie* for the female equivalent and *Nigel* for a nerdy bloke.

Before the bogan, there was the *ocker* and before that there was the *larrikin*. It is interesting that these words start out as derogatory labels but swing around to have some positive value. It is good in Australia to be a bit of a larrikin, and being a bit of an ocker doesn't hurt either. Much better than being *arty-farty*. It seems that *bogan* is similarly upbeat with people commenting that 'there is a little bit of bogan in all of us'. If businessman and politician Clive Palmer is to be believed, we should be proud of it.

Bowerbird

The bowerbird was an intriguing discovery to the European settlers, with its habit of decorating its bower with small blue objects. By the end of the 1800s *bowerbird* became a synonym for 'collector', although usually it was a collector who lacked taste and who collected small colourful objects in a mindless fashion. There was an amusing article that appeared in *The Spectator* and was reprinted in the *Courier-Mail* in 1894 about the bowerbird type of husband:

> *As a matter of fact, all husbands, if they only knew it, are either bower-birds or not bower-birds; but we admit that the phrase is at first sight a little startling, and requires elucidation. It will be remembered that the male bower-bird is endowed by Nature with the desire to decorate its home with every conceivable form of ornament. It is a natural aesthete.*

The article goes on to extend every sympathy to the wife of a bowerbird who fills the house with ornamental clutter.

In the period between the wars *bowerbird* came to mean 'thief' but this focus on the bowerbird's habit of helping itself to whatever object it fancied became less significant as city dwellers had less direct experience of them. At the beginning of the 21st century, the idea of a bowerbird as a collector is still there but the thieving aspect has disappeared. Now, we are more likely to make reference to a bowerbird in a phrase such as *a bit of a bowerbird* or *like a bowerbird* rather than use the word as a direct synonym for 'collector'.

Bush

The word *bush* has a certain significance in Australian English. The dictionary entries go on for pages with *bush* compounds, confirming its key place in our language and culture.

There are subtleties in the use of *bush* that relate to its base range of meanings. The first meaning is the literal one – 'of or relating to the bush', 'found in or suitable for the bush'. So we have compounds like *bush honey* and *bush track*.

There is an added meaning to *bush* and that is 'contrived or put together in an ad-hoc way because of the difficulties of getting the real thing in the bush'. This use of *bush* celebrates Australian inventiveness and adaptability. So we have compounds like *bush bread, bush hut, bush shower*.

The downside of this last meaning, of course, is that what is described as a bush improvisation is crude and unsophisticated, the kind of thing that city slickers would poke fun at. And so we have *bush champagne* (a saline drink with methylated spirits) and *bush pickles* (made by stirring a bottle of Worcestershire sauce into a large tin of plum jam).

Our attitudes to the bush have changed over the centuries. The first colonial citations are full of comments about how hard it is to travel through the bush, how grim it looks, how uncivilised it is. Wild vegetation. Wild and unreclaimed country.

By the end of the century, Banjo Paterson has a different song to sing:

For us the bush is never sad:
Its myriad voices whisper low,
In tones the bushmen only know,
Its sympathy and welcome glad.
For us the roving breezes bring
From many a blossom-tufted tree -
Where wild bees murmur dreamily -
The honey-laden breath of Spring.

From here on, the bush is beautiful but there is an unexpectedly early note of disaster looming in the following 1935 citation: 'The "bush" is the country in its natural state — as it was before men cut down the trees and disturbed its flora and ousted the kangaroo, wallaby, and emu and annihilated the birds that keep our trees healthy'.

Increasingly from this point, any reference to the bush tends to be to a bush remnant or a patch of bush that needs to be preserved. Our thoughts accompany *the bush* with anxiety that we might be losing it, almost as soon as we came to love it.

Then we entered the New Age and, along with the wonderful access to an inner life gained through charms and crystals, we found that spirituality could be enhanced in the bush. I was surprised by a correspondent to a Tasmanian newspaper who recommended that street kids be taken out to camp in some remote spot. He wasn't after some kind of boot camp. He genuinely felt that all that you needed to do with these deprived urban children was to put them in the bush and immediately they would discover a new purpose in life and a connection to an inner peace. You just had to be in the bush to feel that deeper spirituality.

This concept of the healing powers of the bush is also marketable as can be seen from online advertising:

The Australian Bush Flower Essences are borne in the full strength of the Australian sun. ... The ancient wisdom and inherent power of the land, is why the Australian Bush Flower Essences are unique. Therapists and natural health practitioners world

*wide are now incorporating the Australian Bush
Essences to form an integral part of their therapy.*

Or if flower remedies are not your thing:

*This natural treatment is a great way to participate
in a skin treatment that's not designed to be serious.
Following a sand exfoliation on the high tide mark,
you will then cover your skin with the healing
powers of the mangrove mud from Jack's Creek.
Whilst waiting for this to dry you can enjoy a glass
of Australian bubbles before washing off. Mangrove
mud removes toxins from, filters, refreshes, moistens
and softens the skin.*

Or, if we want to take it a little more seriously, we
are invited to consider the proposition that, since
Australia is where the first people on Earth developed
their spirituality in the Dreaming, this will be the
first place on Earth where Satan will want to take
over. It's logical.

It is, however, a long way from the first settlers'
feelings that the bush was untamed and hostile and
not particularly attractive. I know, for instance, how
my grandparents would have reacted to the notion

of luxuriating in the mangrove mud of the Hunter River. Mostly they battled to keep the mud out. The word *bush* is a key item in the Australian lexicon with connotations that have taken some surprising twists and turns.

Capitalisation

The basic rule of capitalisation is that the capital letter conveys the notion of a specific entity as opposed to the lower-case letter, which indicates a generic word, that is, a word for a class or type of items or a member of such a class.

For example, Lake Eyre is capitalised because there is only one lake by that name. On the other hand the lake that you might see in the distance is lower case because you are referring to a feature of the terrain that belongs to the class or type called 'lake'.

There are cases where we become uncertain, often because we are using the specific and the generic in the same context and lose our grip on the difference. So we might be talking politics. There have been a number of prime ministers in Australia but the current Prime Minister is a particular person.

When you start a sentence 'The Prime Minister said today ...', you are using capitals because you are thinking of a specific prime minister of the day. When you talk about the role of the prime minister in Australia, you are talking about the generality of prime ministers.

For this same reason, titles and honorifics are in capitals because they attach to a particular person.

On the education front we may have a student who excels in biology and who is first in the Biology Course Years 7–10 offered by the school. The first use is a field of study – a generic. The second is the name of the very specific course offered by a school.

In all this there are grey areas. 'I love biology' (the field of study) is perilously close to 'I love Biology' (the course at school).

Changing usage

The patterns of language erode over time in much the same way as a rock face weathers away. First it crumbles at the edges as a small trickle of scouring water becomes a flood, then finally whole sections fall away and shatter in the rubble. So too does usage change with small sections of the community adopting the new course. The number of users of the new usage grows until finally all obstacles are cleared and there is wide acceptance in the community.

One of the usages crumbling at the moment is the distinction between *adaptation* and the earlier form *adaption*, with *adaption* the preferred term in the jargon of photography and *adaptation* the preferred term in biological studies. Between those two preferences the two forms are pretty evenly distributed.

With *adaption* and *adaptation* we are dealing with two legitimate variant forms but with the same basic sense, whereas with *sewage* and *sewerage* we have two different words with two different meanings. Perhaps the similarity in sound – just one little indeterminate vowel sound between them – has led to confusion.

There is a fairly solid eroding stream on the distinction between *imply* and *infer*. In this instance, there are those who are still hanging on to the rule that one infers information from the data given. The data on the other hand implies the conclusion. The notion of aspect is a slippery one it seems.

The wall is still holding – *just* – on the use of literally to mean 'in a literal sense'. Yet there is evidence in the writing of the next generation that they see it as an intensifier, a marker of emphasis, and use it in ways that seem ludicrous to the language guardians, as in 'We are literally bending over backwards to address your concerns'. The trickle in this case has almost become a flood.

Cliché dependence

Typesetting used to be done by carving the letters out of a block of wood and then dropping the block into metal that was just cooling, thus creating a metal stereotype from which to print.

The French word for this was *clicher*, a variant of *cliquer* 'to click'. From here we got to the idea that there are some phrases or groups of words that always go together, as if they have been fixed in hot metal.

We use clichés in the same way that we use 'um' and 'you know' – as conversation fillers that give us a little bit more time to think about the next thing we are going to say. Our poor little brains need to keep one step ahead of our mouths or else, as many public figures know, there can be a disaster.

It is true – and I think that we all resent this – how quickly we drift into clichés. Your mind is hurtling down a sentence anticipating the word 'event' and, before you know it, 'memorable' has inserted itself glibly with a smooth inevitability that, in retrospect, you find appalling. It requires constant vigilance to guard against what seems to be the brain's default system. (Looking back at that sentence I wonder if I can get away with 'constant vigilance'. At least it wasn't 'eternal'.)

There is, however, one kind of cliché that seems to have a positive function as a de facto technical language. These words are not so much clichés as formulaic expressions that have been given an agreed meaning over time within a specialised context. The language of wine labels is, for example, full of these repeated words and phrases that attempt to pin down our sense of taste. The label in front of me talks about 'complex character' and 'spice' and 'the full spectrum of fruit flavours'. It mentions both 'berries' and 'plum'. It comments on the 'natural tannins' that 'lengthen the palate'. The combinations of these hammered out bits of wine patter are meaningful to the cognoscenti and are the best they can do under the circumstances, flavours being extremely difficult to describe in any objective way.

Sports writers are equally required to balance the startling and original metaphor, the one that will make the headline, against the by-common-consent cliché. Whoever thought up the expression 'grinding game' for football has been rewarded by its acceptance in the jargon of the code's followers. A football commentator can hardly avoid using this or, by contrast, 'free-flowing play', because it quickly and accurately sets the scene for the reader.

Politics is another area where clichés abound. I approve of our politicians being diligent and energetic in the pursuit of their goals, which are our goals, but I do wish former prime minister Kevin Rudd didn't 'roll up his sleeves' quite so often. Three times in one announcement is a bit excessive. There does seem to be a rhetorical strategy involved here, that the repetition of a somewhat old-fashioned cliché will engender trust. Perhaps it failed because he didn't go quite far enough. Three times was merely irritating but six times would have reduced me to a sentimental mush. It is important when creating an effect to make it clear to the audience that it is intended. I hadn't thought of the cliché as a device to be used in this way, but if there are those of us who respond at an emotional level to alphabetical order, then manipulating the feel-good factor of the cliché should be a snack.

Clichés are also fashion statements. It is good to be in the vanguard of those who know the smartest coolest thing to say but then the mob follows and we are all saying it. 'Absolutely' was so fashionable and now we beat ourselves over the head with a stick if we find ourselves still saying it. At least, I do.

Conversely there are groups who use clichés deliberately to identify each other as belonging to the same tribe. If you find yourself with someone who can, with confidence, use expressions like *drill down* and *get some leverage* and *unpack this idea* then you know that you have found someone who can talk the talk and therefore, conceivably, walk the walk.

After we have used a phrase for a while we no longer split it into its separate elements. We take the meaning of the phrase as a whole. In the case of well-worn phrases it can be disconcerting to pause to think about them. In many instances we no longer know what the literal meaning is and are therefore puzzled, or amused, as our imaginations try to come up with an explanation. Just contemplate a phrase like *no room to swing a cat!* (By the by, the best guess about this phrase is that it does refer to a real cat. It is a 1650s joke in Britain that doesn't seem so funny now. There are lots of other guesses, the most popular one being that it is a reference to the cat o' nine tails on board a ship. Feel free to speculate.)

Clichés are defended in speech on the grounds that in such improvised communication we cannot be original all the time. Off-the-shelf expressions speed up the process of assembling our thoughts. But in writing, where so much of the extra communicativeness of speech is denied, imperfections in the text turn the reader's mind away from the meaning to the surface form. For this reason I would put clichés in the same category as misspellings, oddities of syntax, too much punctuation or too little, all of which amount to surface noise. Our minds reject with impatience any wads of verbiage from which all meaning has leached out over time. And the fragile thread that binds the writer and the reader is broken.

Better to be pretty than to be clever

The word *clever* in Australian usage can often come close to meaning 'too clever by half'. In school to be a clever kid won you some acknowledgement but by no means meant that you were trusted or liked. I turned to Ozcorp, our corpus of Australian writing, for instances of *clever* that would shed some light and almost immediately came on confirmation of my impression that, whereas in everyone else's English *clever* has bright, positive connotations, in Australian English it shades off into darkness fairly rapidly. Take Frank Dalby Davison with Young Harry who had been a shade too clever in flaunting a stolen horse with a fake brand right under the noses of the police, and who was later described as 'a quite clever inventor of impromptu fictions'. Then Blanche d'Alpuget with 'those clever university girls who married External Affairs men'. And Clive James whose 'clever lip won me whatever popularity was coming to me at the time'. These are all comments tinged with disdain. Most damning of all is

Patrick White whose character Chattie sums up Laura Trevalyn: '"Laura is sweet, too," Chattie sighed. "But peculiar. Laura is clever."'

All of which confirms my feeling that to be clever in Australian schools, in Australian society, is a compliment tinged with contempt. To be clever enough to do something, to be clever at something, even to be a clever lad, this is all okay. But to be accused of unadorned, unqualified, uncontextualised cleverness is to be set aside as a doubtful quantity.

Curriculums or curricula?

The rules of language are not absolutes but rather summaries of patterns occurring at particular times. Confusions arise when the patterns of one language are applied to another, as when English grammarians tried to make English conform to Latin rules, or when a rule that did apply in English at one time hangs on as an anachronism. 'Correctness' can therefore vary from one period to another and from one person to another, depending on their allegiances to particular patterns.

The other aspect of language that affects these patterns is our attitude to 'borrowed' words. When these are first taken into our language we are much more conscious of their origin than we are a few centuries later, so time is a factor. Also the degree of assimilation matters – are we constantly reminded by the look of a word that it is ultimately foreign or is its form completely anglicised? The position of the word in the lexicon matters as well – is it a word in general use or is it part of a more specialised vocabulary where there might be a greater tendency to remember its past?

Curriculum is at the centre of a contemporary tug-of-war between a Latin way of forming plurals and an English way. It is one of a set of words that have shifted to the English way of doing things without much question. I don't know that many people talk about *aquaria* or *condominia* and the enthusiasm for *gymnasia* is definitely waning.

There are still some words in the set, however, where some of the other factors that I mentioned apply. The word *curriculum* is a central term in education jargon so there are people who see it as important to education to remember where *curriculum* has come from and what plural form was thought proper. If the teachers can't get it right, how will the children get a decent education? Similarly, *ova* is retained in medical jargon because of the conservatism surrounding the use of scientific words. And there is a divergence of opinion on *referendums* and *referenda* in political circles.

I would think that most people in education would think that literacy is not dependent on a changing fashion in English grammar that relates to a small set of words. On the contrary *curricula* and its mates would constitute the kind of trap for young players that they would prefer to dismiss so that they can deal with more pressing problems. But I am not an education expert, so this is merely speculation on my part. Whatever their view, I am sure that the goal of education is to teach the standards of the community, so if our educators saw *curriculums* as being unacceptable to the language community they would not use it and they would not teach it.

From my point of view as a lexicographer I would say that the tide has turned on these words, at least in the general domain, and that while there may be a few who cling to *curricula* and *referenda*, the vast majority prefer to regard this set as properly assimilated into English and taking English plurals.

On a simple count in a number of large databases of text, it is clear that *curricula* and *referenda* form a small minority. A citation for *gymnasia* is increasingly rare. *Vacua* cannot be found anywhere. So the trend is clear.

At the moment however it is still the case that *curriculums* and *curricula*, *referendums* and *referenda*, are acceptable variants within the community. So *curricula* is as correct, that is, considered to be as much standard usage by the language community, as *curriculums*. It is up to each individual to decide what their preference is. And whatever their preference is, they should be allowed to use it. Equally they should be respectful of the legitimate choices made by others.

Derogatory terms

These are the new taboo words and can be dangerous territory, especially when they are colloquialisms. Especially when they are colloquial ways of calling someone an idiot or worse. Mark Latham got into trouble with *skanky ho* and Peter Costello raised a few eyebrows with *dropkick*. A John Laws eyebrow to be specific, because Laws can remember the starting point of this term which is *dropkick and punt*, rhyming slang for ... You guessed it. The term *dropkick* has taken on pretty much all the meanings that the c-word has, referring as it does to an unpleasant or stupid person, or a device or machine that won't work. The earliest citation we have for it is a collection of rhyming slang published in 1983.

I could sense a certain amount of scepticism from John Laws when I made the point in Costello's defence that it is part of the pattern of rhyming slang that after a certain interval of time the rhyme is shortened. For those in the know this is a sweet moment because they and they alone appreciate what lies behind the word. The danger is that the rest of us pick up the term, knowing what it means in contemporary slang but not where it came from.

Indeed, I suspect that folk etymologising has come into play with this word. It sounds harmless and the meaning has focused on 'idiot' rather than 'contemptible person'. Maybe, not knowing our football, we even visualise someone clumsily dropping the ball and miskicking it. Certainly *dropkick* is regarded as a fairly amiable insult whereas the c-word is the ultimate taboo.

So Costello can be accused of not being in on rhyming slang. Since not many of us form the habit of this arcane way of speaking, that is not surprising. Latham on the other hand picked up a piece of slang that was, broadly speaking, an insult to a woman, the precise meaning of which escaped him. He accused a journalist of being a *skanky ho*, an item of Black American English which roughly translates as 'dirty whore'. His excuse for his ignorance was that, as a fan of Meatloaf, he wasn't up with rap music.

Of course everyone remembers Paul Keating and his use of *scumbag* – but I suspect that Keating always knew exactly what he meant.

Dictionary imitates life

In 2008 the new word list for the update of the dictionary was awash with *green, eco-, emission* and *carbon* compounds. We acquired words like *green house* (an environmentally friendly house) and *green roof* (a roof with a covering of vegetation), *eco-activism* and *eco-warrior, emissions trading market* and *emission permit, carbon sequestration* and *carbon capture.* We would have had an environment-led update if it had not been for the GFC with its attendant flurry of lexical items.

Other aspects of society are still producing the odd notable addition to the dictionary. Online we have taken to *lifestreaming,* which allows us to view the intimate boring detail of someone else's day-to-day activities. The blog has produced the *flog* (an advertising blog) and the *splog* (a blog simply designed to up the frequency rating of a website). These were quickly followed by the *celeblog* (celebrity + blog), the *microblog,* the *moblog* (mobile + blog), and the *mummy blog.* We are concerned about *helicopter parenting* (obsessively protective parenting) and amused at those who have *fur children* (adored pets) and take courses in *pet parenting*. We are wearing *pussybow blouses* and *mouth grills* (diamond-studded gold braces), the girls sporting *cocktail rings* and the boys *pimp cups*. Our schools have *electronic whiteboards* and our streets have *PODS* (Parking Overstay Detection Systems, i.e., a more efficient way of issuing parking fines). We are undertaking *agritourism, battlefield tourism, connoisseur tourism, dark tourism* (tourism directed towards sites of death and disaster, often for the purpose of remembrance or education), *dental care tourism, destination tourism, drug tourism, ecotourism, fertility tourism, space tourism, suicide tourism, transplant tourism, tech-free tourism, voluntourism, war tourism* and *wellness tourism*. Who says dictionaries don't tell us about ourselves?

Digger

The first specialised use of *digger* in Australian English was a reference to someone digging for gold in a goldfield and dates back to the 1850s gold rush in Victoria. This use carried on through the century right up to the goldfields rush in Western Australia in the 1890s. When Australian and New Zealand soldiers went to World War I in France and were introduced to trench warfare, the term *digger* perhaps came more naturally than the British *sapper*. These were privates who earned this name, the soldiers at the frontline who actually did the digging, but the use spread until it encompassed all Australian and New Zealand soldiers of any rank and was used as a form of greeting. Prime Minister Billy Hughes was affectionately nicknamed the 'Little Digger' by the Australian troops he visited in France. In World War II the term was restricted to Australian soldiers.

It was a term that meant a great deal to those who fought in World War I, and who had very clear notions of who was a digger and who wasn't, notions which have become blurred over time. This writer to the Bulletin in 1922 was attempting to keep the record straight:

> *'Digger' is a title coveted and often stolen. It originally meant the infantryman or artilleryman who was always 'digging' or rebuilding his parapet after enemy fire … It did not mean a staff-officer or any of the AIF serving in Palestine or Egypt. It meant the man in the front line in France, and no one else. It is ridiculous to talk of the 'Digger Prince' or to use the word for AIF men indiscriminately; and it is mere swank when claimed by men who did not dig. There were no 'Diggers' at Gallipoli where we dug most – the word had not come then!*

I fear that usage swept aside all these nice distinctions.

How to shed the digital overdose

At first I thought that *digital detox* was something that the older generation craved. Some respite from all the devices that now crowd our lives combined with a memory that it was not always so and that, from this distance, the digital-free world seems better, nobler.

It turns out that it is the craving of all those at work who want to shed their mobile phones and iPads when they go on holiday so that they truly cannot be contacted. It's not their fault. They don't have to make a decision about whether to check their emails or not. They are in a dead zone and it's just not possible.

So we have the rise of *tech-free tourism*. Some resorts that offer this are of the opinion that nature and the digital world are ideologically and aesthetically opposed. Going back to nature cannot be accomplished with a smart phone in the hand. (I don't actually agree with that – GPS availability can be very reassuring to the bushwalker. The facility to photograph and record what you see can be good too, although the downside of that is obsessive documenting.)

Other resorts have sensed this need for a refuge from the digital. There is no religious zeal. You can eat, drink, walk, swim, study astronomy, go rafting, do a whole heap of different things just for the fun of it, but you will not be troubled by nagging guilt or anxiety once you have been forced to shed the devices.

Dead zones and wellbeing have been studied by academics (wouldn't that be a fun thesis topic?) and stress levels correlated with exposure to mobile phones. Positive experiences were linked with loss of contact with work but also with loved ones! The 'acca' coinage was *dead zone tourism*, which could conceivably be misinterpreted. The accepted term is *tech-free tourism*, which seems to be expanding as a profitable venture. The list of 'tourisms', already extensive, has added one more.

Dining boom

I find this a witty coinage. Thinking it logical to start with the word *boom*, I began with the word's etymology, not expecting any problems. I had assumed that *boom* derived from the association with a sudden explosion. Things that boomed went off with a bang. It seems, however, that *boom* in the sense of a sudden burst of economic growth and prosperity is clearly an Americanism of the 1870s and follows on from an American slang expression (early 1880s) that had its starting point in ships. When they reached full speed, the sails made a booming noise as the wind caught them and they became taut. This gave rise to a meaning of *boom*, to hurry at top speed, to *boom along*. Things other than people could also boom, that is, suddenly develop at great speed. The expression *boom and bust* appeared in the US the 1940s.

The first specific kind of boom was a land boom, as can be seen in this quote from the *Kilmore Free Press* (Victoria) 1882:

LAND SPECULATION IN THE UNITED STATES

Enormous fortunes are being made in the United States by the buying and selling of land in 'booming' districts. A striking instance of this is afforded by the speculators in land incident to the founding of a new city in the midst of the Pennsylvania wilderness. Previous to the founding of the 'city' land within what was now its boundaries could be had for 9d an acre. Recently the district was found to abound with oil; the news of the 'boom' was flashed all over the North American Continent, and in less than three weeks land rose from the 'old song' of 9d an acre to the respectable figure, of £200 an acre. Already the new town is full of stores and hotels, the telegraph and the telephone has been laid on, and everybody there is making a fortune.

By the early 1900s we had a *mining boom* linked specifically to the stock exchange. There have been others – a *rubber boom*, a *cotton boom*, etc. But now we have capped all this with the *dining boom*. This coinage cleverly captures the idea that it is not bulk wheat we are talking about here, but upmarket produce destined for the flourishing restaurants in China catering for the expanding middle class. It positions this enterprise somewhat pugnaciously against the mining boom as the hope of the future for Australia. When the mining boom is bust, the business of supplying the dining tables of Asia will be going strong.

Disgraced words

I wonder if we should have a special form of presentation in the dictionary for words that have been up to no good, have got themselves into trouble in some way, and come home to their editors in disgrace? I am referring to a word like *economic rationalism*. Perhaps we could rim the entry with a black border, or we could set up a special corner of an appendix where naughty words could sit until such time as they redeem themselves.

In the case of *economic rationalism* such redemption seems unlikely since it has taken a dark turn and become extreme capitalism. This uses the old-fashioned sense of extreme meaning 'going too far', rather than the new meaning of 'dangerously exciting' as in extreme sports and extreme programming. So dark are the times that a return to the dour use of language is appropriate. It is reminiscent of Cato the Elder adjuring the population of Rome with such timely reminders as 'Cessation of work is not accompanied by cessation of expenses'. Only too true we say as we all look askance at what happened to our superannuation.

But to return to the global verbal crisis, let us refresh our memories on *economic rationalism* and its peculiarly Australian meaning. Rationalism in the context of economics has a history that dates back in British English to the end of the 20th century and was a term most often used to indicate that the world could be made better by the application of some rational thinking to the natural instincts of the financial jungle. An economic rationalist would on that basis be assumed to favour more intervention rather than less.

The Australian use of the term would seem to relate rationalism to rationalise rather than to reason, advocating, as it did, the stripping away of all those controls and encumbrances that hamper the economy from operating purely according to its own laws. The dictionary definition is 'a theory of economics which opposes government intervention and which maintains that the economy of a country works better when it responds to marketplace forces in such matters as venture planning and industrial relations' (*Macquarie Dictionary*). Our economic rationalist believes in less intervention rather than more.

But oh, the shame of it — to be now branded as extreme capitalism, the cause of the credit crunch (not a new term but a revival). *Golden handshake* can join it in the corner, as can *paper profits*. Suddenly, to be making too much money earns a disapproving shake of the head.

It has been interesting to see the way in which the Australian community baulked at the American use of the Main Street as the metaphor for the consumption of real products for real money in opposition to Wall Street as the centre of paper money and paper profits. Similarly, although we have become familiar with the British use of High Street, as in *high-street retailers*, we don't warm to it. Our media carefully selected *the real economy* instead. We have, however, accepted the use of *perfect storm* and been schooled in the understanding of a *moral hazard*. But the most surprising outcome of the *GFC* (our term in preference to *credit crunch*) has been the brief use of *Icelandic* to mean 'dodgy'.

When English became Englishes

In 1981 the first edition of the *Macquarie Dictionary* was published with an entry for *English*. In 1991 this word *English* had acquired a plural form *Englishes* and a rewrite of its definitions to allow for English to refer to any one of the varieties of English spoken around the world, such as Australian English, South African English, American English and, to put us all on an equal footing, British English. The linguist associated with introducing the notion of the plurality of Englishes is Braj Kachru and he had quite some difficulty getting this key concept past his editor.

Just as the dream of universal English beckons, we are alerted to the threat of disintegration yet again. The Tower of Babel revisited.

The notion of universality took a late 20th century twist in the form of International English or World English, which is sometimes taken to mean a functional distillation of that which is common to all the Englishes. If I were addressing an international audience I would abandon phrases like *shoot through like a Bondi tram* or even items like *home unit* or *removalist* on the basis that these would not be a part of the international lexicon.

There are hesitant attempts to smooth out the written form of International English as well. In practice this means the removal of the distinctions between British and American spelling, the adjustment of which presently takes up so much of our time so needlessly.

Unfortunately self-image lies not just in the choices we make of the words we like to use, but also in the way in which we like to spell them. As speakers of a minor variety of English, Australians have taken a stance on British and American spellings. British spelling is our past, American spelling may well be our future but we are not rushing to get there. There are those who resist American spelling as a token of their opposition to American culture. Equally, there are those who feel that a bit of Americanism is a necessary indicator of modernity and stylishness.

Singaporeans have much the same attitude to Americanisms as we do, but Thai English speakers are refreshingly unconcerned about spelling variation. British teaching materials used to be popular so British spelling was common, but now American textbooks have greater appeal, so American spelling is the norm.

Of course this cheerful insensitivity comes from the fact that they are learning English as a foreign language. They are making very limited choices themselves as a community and have no particular attachments or allegiances but just do what they are told is best by those who know. Nevertheless, it opens up the possibility of a world that is not quite so relentlessly carved up into British English or American English domains, a world in which our colonial heritages don't appear quite so obvious.

At the moment the dictionaries are at the stage of telling us that, for international purposes, either system of spelling will do. *Color* or *colour* will both be counted as correct. However, we haven't yet reached the point where we will accept a document that has *colour* but *favor*, *realise* but *rationalize*. We may have reached the point where we can accept either system, but we look for consistency.

The concept of International English is a nebulous one because there is not a community of speakers of this variety – just speakers of regional varieties who happen to meet in an international forum. So it exists only as a slight modification to each particular regional variety. As greater numbers of English speakers divide their lives into home and away zones – by travel, by email, by allegiance to international organisations – perhaps the sense of an international community will grow stronger and the flow-on in terms of the shaping of an international dialect of English will become more apparent.

Softly, softly – the euphemism

There is a special category of euphemism that we now call 'code words' where the intention is not so much to block from our minds the taboo reference because it is so shocking but to soften the blow. It is a matter of etiquette. We wish not to confront our listeners or readers with something too blunt so we collectively hit on a form of words that everyone will understand but which will not give offence. For example, *confirmed bachelor* has long been understood to mean 'homosexual'. To be *tired and emotional* is to be drunk. I am quite fond of the use of *troubled* in the ABC's news style. Whenever a state or community is troubled you know there are people out there with meat axes. We can breathe a sigh of relief when the *troubled* epithet is dropped and life resumes something approaching normal.

When people are troubled they are suffering some malaise of the spirit. When places are troubled they are the locus of trouble, so a *troubled residence* is one that the ambulance officers visit only with police escort. We have *troubled addresses*, *troubled nursing homes*, *troubled psych wards*, and, of course, *the troubled province of Aceh*, which is thankfully not experiencing trouble at the moment and so can be referred to simply as Aceh.

An old favourite among these expressions, although one with rather more point to it, is a *colourful racing identity*, which is clearly understood to be a reference to a criminal. By the late 1800s the term *colourful*, applied to things other than paint or clothes, meant 'lively and full of interest'. From here it was a small move to the euphemistic use, as in 'to lead a colourful life'. *Colourful language* was swearing. The link to racing came about because in the early 20th century the racecourse was one of the few legitimate places to gamble and so provided the most common means of money laundering. Meanwhile journalists were hemmed in by Australian defamation laws and needed to have a safe formula to identify people involved in such practices. And so the *colourful racing identity* was born.

Events of significance

It is interesting to see how the community forges names for events that have some significance, locally or globally, as, for example, the *Petrov affair*, the *Tampa crisis*, the *loans affair* and *children overboard affair*. Sometimes different communities arrive at different names. We chose *September 11*, the Americans *9/11*. We all seem to have agreed on *Boxing Day tsunami*. In terms of the dictionary, they each present a special case. Sometimes the agreed term is clear, but in other cases it is fuzzy. The *Tampa crisis* could just as easily be the *Tampa affair*, the *Tampa incident*. At the moment we are uncertain as to the wording of *turn-the-boats-back policy* or *turn-the-boats-around policy*. The argument for including them in an encyclopedic dictionary is that they are important landmarks in our cultural landscape, they are agreed collocations (more or less) that the community uses to reference those landmarks and, last but not least, that it is useful to the user of the dictionary to have that information.

Cultural landmarks have the added unusual feature that they can sometimes have the stability of the

Cheshire Cat's grin. Are terms like the *Axis of Evil* and the *Coalition of the Willing* real, in the sense they have achieved common use, or are they just the product of a particular spin? Some people would argue that they are solid items of reference; others would deny them existence entirely. It would seem from looking at their patterns of use that it is possible for non-propagandists to use them with some sense of what their content of meaning is. So, after much discussion, they go into the dictionary. Again, the utilitarian argument wins the day.

Etymology as fact
or fiction

Talkback radio is the conduit par excellence for modern folktales and provides me with the interesting story about the daddy-long-legs spider whose venom is so powerful that it can kill a human being several times over. This little spider would be feared greatly except for the fact that it is too small to wrap its fangs around a juicy human being. Large in venom, but small in bite. The irony appeals to us – the little spider that could have ruled the world if only …

Folk etymologies are similar stories but about the origins of words. Their appeal lies in the way they seem to fit the meaning of the word in a way that seems profound. There is something in us that rebels from the notion of a language as a conglomeration of happenstance. We like to feel that there is direction, that words develop meanings in an orderly fashion.

It is a fact of language that although we don't always know where words have come from, this doesn't in any way handicap our contemporary use of them.

Even today when our ability to document language, to archive texts, to search enormous amounts of data in tracing the history of words is so greatly increased, we are stymied by the fact that many words began their lives in the spoken language, where they go mostly unrecorded. By the time these words turn up in print the nexus between the word and the idea that inspired its origin is often broken.

The history of Australian English is short by comparison with the broader history of the English language, but even so we have our mysteries. One of these was the word *kangaroo*, a word so important to our history and culture that it could not possibly go unexplained. The first mention of the word was in the diaries of James Cook where he recounted a meeting with the Aborigines at Endeavour River. A kangaroo bounced past. Cook asked the Aborigines what it was – he hadn't seen one before. The Aborigines said: *Kangaroo*.

The only problem was that no one, as time went on, could track the word down in the local Aboriginal language. That may say something about the state of research into Aboriginal languages in Australia at that time. Ignorance created a vacuum that folk etymology filled. In one story, the Aborigines misunderstood

Cook and gave him the name of something else on the landscape. In others, they understood perfectly but, joking at his expense, gave him a rude word instead. Ultimately all this was sorted out by the linguists. Cook's account was validated but the story still lingers.

Another folktale deals with the origin of *fair dinkum*. It is supposed that 'dinkum' is a Cantonese expression meaning true gold and comes from the excited cry of Chinese on the goldfields when they struck it rich. The Europeans picked the word up in that linguistic cross-fertilisation that occurred when all manner of people were thrown together in the camaraderie of the gold rushes.

The origin of *dinkum* actually lies in British dialect, where it meant 'a day's allocation of work'. Your dinkum was what you were required to get done, so naturally a *fair dinkum* was a matter of some importance. The phrase *fair dinkum* existed in the Lincolnshire dialect.

Didjeridu is not an Aboriginal word but a white man's imitation of the sound given a pseudo-Aboriginal spelling. *News* is not an acronym for north, east, west, south but a nominalisation of the adjective *new*. *Wog* is not from *worthy oriental gentleman* or even *western oriental gentleman*. Its origin is unknown.

And so it goes. By the way, it is as I suspected. The humble daddy-long-legs could barely poison a fly, let alone a human being.

Fiji English

Friday, 20 October 2006 was a momentous day in Fiji. Yes, they were about to host the Pacific Islands Forum. Yes, the Supreme Court was about to decide the constitutional role of the military. But something else happened on that day that will endure in Fiji history, and that was the launch of the *Macquarie Dictionary of English for the Fiji Islands*. As Prime Minister Laisenia Qarase said:

> *We have taken the English language inherited from our colonial past and turned it into something of our own, something that's dynamic and colourful and accurately reflects the way of life unique to the people of our island.*

It was strange for me to experience again on a smaller scale all the emotions I felt when the *Macquarie Dictionary* was first published in 1981. Only in the tiny island of Fiji have we been able to get the same mix of emotional investment in a variety of English, community support and the basic lexicography that has enabled us to produce this dictionary.

In Singapore and Malaysia, and in the Philippines, where the local varieties are just as strong, where the contributions to English have been just as great, there are barriers. Governments refuse to acknowledge their own kind of English. The communities are divided in their support of it, some being passionately attached to their English, others opposing it with equal vigour as a corruption of the language. Education departments reel in shock at the notion that some words of the local English might legitimately appear in a dictionary. No dictionary publishing of the local variety is possible in a hostile environment.

In Fiji, the PM launched the dictionary, *The Fiji Times* supported it, and the University of the South Pacific in Suva was delighted to host the occasion. Another variety of English was proudly documented in its own dictionary.

Then there was the coup and everything changed again, but for one brief moment ...

The Flash Language

The first record of Australian English was an account of convict language, brought to the colony by the thieves of London and generally referred to as 'the Flash Language'. James Hardy Vaux, a convict himself, defined *flash* as the cant language used by the 'family'. To speak 'good flash' is to be well versed in cant terms. Although there is no clear knowledge of the origin of the term *flash*, the suggestion is that it referred to a specific district between Buxton Leek and Macclesford in northern England.

A *flash-man*, to quote Vaux again, was:

'a favourite or fancy-man; *but this term is generally applied to those dissolute characters upon the town, who subsist upon the liberality of unfortunate women; and who, in return, are generally at hand during their nocturnal perambulations, to protect them should any brawl occur, or should they be detected in robbing those whom they have* picked up'.

A flash-man was a pimp, in other words.

Vaux (or his editor) italicises 'picked up' to show that this is a flash term also. So we turn to the entry in Vaux's dictionary to discover that *to pick someone up* has a broader sense than we are used to and means:

> *to accost, or enter into conversation with any person, for the purpose of executing some design upon his personal property; thus, among gamblers, it is called* picking up a flat *[honest man], or a* mouth *[foolish person]:* sharpers *[swindlers], who are daily on the look-out for some unwary country-man or stranger, use the same phrase; and among* drop-coves, *and others who act in concert, this task is allotted to one of the gang, duly qualified, who is thence termed* the picker-up; *and he having performed his part, his associates proceed systematically in* cleaning out the flat. *To* pick up a cull, *is a term used by* blowens *[prostitutes] in their vocation of street-walking. To* pick *a person* up, *in a general sense, is to impose upon, or take advantage of him, in a contract or bargain.*

While we have lost that general sense of taking advantage, we are left with picking someone up for the purpose of sex. The phrase for us has become more limited in context.

The following are words that Vaux records as 'Flash Language' with which we would be familiar today:

> *awake to something* aware of what's going on
> *old chum/new chum* originally referring to
>   fellow prisoners in a jail or hulk
> *do the trick* originally referring to a
>   successfully accomplished robbery or
>   other such illegal business
> *fence* receiver of stolen goods
> *frisk* search
> *gammon* deceit, pretence, plausible language
> *kid* young child, especially a boy who
>   thieves at an early age (perhaps
>   explaining the opprobrium in which this
>   word is held by many)
> *plant* something hidden or concealed
> *racket* particular kind of fraud
> *on the sly* secretly
> *snitch on someone* tell on someone
> *sting* swindle
> *swag* bundle
> *turn up trump* be fortunate
> *wack* share

Vaux claimed that he wrote his Vocabulary to help officialdom in the colony – magistrates and gaolers – understand what was being said by the convicts.

It seems as likely that it was produced with the sense that this was one way of capturing the colour of the colonial environment, that it was publishable material back in London. Whatever the reason, Vaux demonstrated that he had the instincts of a lexicographer. His collection is a valuable record of one formative influence on Australian English.

Forgotten and misunderstood

There are phrases that were perfectly well understood when they were first uttered but which, over time, have come to be misconstrued, usually because there is a word in the phrase that has become obsolete. One example of this is *a wigwam for a goose's bridle*. This should be *a whimwham for a goose's bridle*, a *whimwham* being an ornament or decoration. It is a word that dates back to the 15th century, a humorous reduplication of *whim* possibly related to *whimsical*, but it is now obsolete. It is intriguing that we seem not to tolerate words that we don't know at all, preferring to replace them with a word that has a vague resemblance in sound although not in sense whatsoever. But then in this case the whole phrase is meant to be nonsensical. Whoever heard of putting a bridle on a goose and decorating it! It is deliberate nonsense intended to deflect a question or comment that we do not wish to answer.

Another example is one that causes more trouble these days, *one fell swoop*. In this case the word *fell* meaning 'savage, cruel, fierce' is the word that has dropped out of fashion. I wouldn't say that it is entirely obsolete but it entered the realms of rather old-fashioned poetic diction. The word comes into English from Old French from Italian, and ultimately from popular Latin. Initially it referred to natural agents such as disease or suffering, and came from a Latin word for cholera. The *fell swoop* is the savage swoop of a bird of prey. Unfortunately when this is changed to *foul swoop* the image is not quite so affecting and once it becomes *fowl swoop*, it is positively ludicrous. Again we prefer the word we know to the one that mystifies us.

Another -*gate* to add to the collection

It is always interesting to see the intuitive decision-making on what the suffix -*gate* should attach itself to in the formation of -*gate* coinages. Sometimes it is easy – remember *Keelgate*, the scandal that erupted around Ben Lexcen's controversial keel as the New York Yacht Club sought to have it declared illegal? The choice there was obvious – the keel was the problem. When there are people involved, we tend to deflect the focus of our attention to something else that gives us the cue without directly linking scandal to any individual unless they are in a position where they would find it difficult to fight back, as in *Monicagate*. In the case of *Iguanagate* this lateral manoeuvre worked well. The image of the disgraced lizard didn't hurt either party.

It is always interesting when a political scandal erupts to see where the -*gate* suffix will land. In 2009, during the OzCar affair, Prime Minister Kevin Rudd was clearly the target of the Leader of the Opposition Malcolm Turnbull's outrage but *Ruddgate* was not what emerged as the label for this particular storm in a car yard. Possibly that was because *Ruddgate* had been used up when it was applied to the suggested malpractices of Rudd's wife in supposedly siphoning off government money into her business. But I think in the end it was just that *Utegate* was more appealing. No one ever suggested *Godwingate* or *Grechgate*.

We have been very restrained with -*gate* in the dictionary, listing just *Watergate* and the suffix itself. I suppose that this is because none of the particular -*gates* that have come and gone have been sufficiently effective in claiming a political scalp at a national level. *Utegate* was interesting in that it very nearly claimed the scalp of the 'gater' rather than the 'gatee'. But we still wait for the big one that will take its own special place in the dictionary wordlist.

Gotten

In Australian English, *gotten* was traditionally regarded as a crude and ignorant dialectism. But now increasingly *gotten* is seeping into our English. There is a distinction maintained between *got* for obligation ('You've got to do it') and possession ('He has got the prize') and *gotten* for becoming or achieving ('He has gotten very wealthy'). For some Australians it is an instant marker of American English and therefore an instant reject, but for others it is increasingly the norm. In terms of frequency, *gotten* appeared in our newspaper database roughly 300 times in the early 1980s, 500 times in the early 1990s and 800 times in the late 1990s. Our style guides still regard *gotten* as perfectly correct in American English but as raising an eyebrow in Australian English. How long this editorial eyebrow will remain raised is anyone's guess. I feel that *gotten* will reach at least the level of acceptable variation very soon.

Honour and honor

It might seem simply that *honour* is following a spelling rule, on the pattern of *rigour/rigorous, humour/ humorous*, etc., where the nouns include a *u* in British English and the adjectives dispense with it. At various times, all such adjectives have been spelled with a *u* – with the exception of *glamorous*, which is much more recent than the others and fell into step from its inception.

The story of *honour* is a muddle. English imported it via the Anglo-Norman *onour*, itself a respelling of the older French forms *onor* and *onur*. The earliest Middle English spelling was *anour*. The *h* has never been sounded but was inserted early in its English history by scholars who knew its Latin source was *honor*, 'repute' or 'esteem', and felt that its English descendent ought to be spelled to match. *Honour, honourable* and *honorary* have been lumbered with that unnecessary initial letter ever since.

Common forms in the 1500s, before standardisation of spelling, were *honur, honor* and *honour*. Shakespeare used both *honor* and *honour* but preferred *honor. Honour* became usual in the 17th century but the pendulum swung back in the 18th century. John Ash had it as *honor* in his *New and Complete Dictionary of the English Language* in 1775, and commented that it was 'a modern but correct spelling, from the Latin'. Less than two decades later, John Wesley, the founder of Methodism, recommended instead that preachers should 'Avoid the fashionable impropriety of leaving out the *u* in many words, as *honor*, *vigor*, &c. This is mere childish affectation'. His advice seems to have been prescient, since *honour* has been so spelled in Britain pretty much ever since.

The story of *honorary* is of similar confusion. At its inception in the 17th century it was spelled without a *u*. There was a period in the 18th century when the *u*-form became fashionable, weirdly around the time that people were leaving it out of *honour*. In his *Universal Etymological English Dictionary* of 1733, Nathan Bailey thought the *u*-less form the better spelling but recommended *honourary* because it was then more usual. By the century's end, the fashion had abated again and we've spelled *honorary* without the *u* ever since.

The spelling reforms of Noah Webster in the US that led to the loss of the *u* in *honour* in that country in effect returned that word to a spelling that had been common in England for several centuries. If only he had gone the whole hog and removed the *h* as well.

How do words get into the dictionary?

This is a common question from the users of the dictionary. Of all the countless words that are flung around the world each day, how is it that some are admitted to the select group encompassed by the dictionary headword list?

The test for inclusion is always currency, within the whole community or within a section of it. If enough people know the word and use it as a token of meaningful exchange, then it ought to be in the dictionary. Finding evidence of this comes down to finding instances of a word's use from a variety of sources over a reasonable period of time – say five years. This second test ensures that a word has a permanent place in our English and isn't just a one-day or one-year wonder. We all know words that the media have picked up, tossed around like brightly coloured balls and then abandoned.

For all the words that are in the dictionary there are in fact many more that could be there, particularly words from specialist activities. The jargon associated with computers could go on forever so the editor of a general dictionary has to decide how much of it the average writer or reader or computer user is likely to come across in their lives. Similarly the jargon of skateboarding is extensive, but while it has high currency among skateboard riders, how much of it should be included in a general dictionary? Again, general currency is the test. Who would have heard of the term *moral hazard* until the governments of the world started discussing whether or not they should bail out the banks and what the terms of such a bailout should be? The discussion is faithfully reported in our newspapers and the term is included in the dictionary for those who might wish to get a better handle on it.

The dictionary's reach should also extend into the past to those words that once had currency but that no longer do so. The ghosts of these words still drift across contemporary life, particularly in our reading of earlier periods of literature. And where should the reader turn for an explanation if not to his or her dictionary?

How does a word come to the attention of the dictionary editors? There are lots of fish in this verbal sea but how do the fishers of words get them into the net?

There is a low-tech way and a high-tech way. The low-tech way is the way of Dr Johnson and of other dictionary editors in the past. The editors read, and listen, and make a record of anything interesting that they find. Words like those included in the dictionary online have been gathered by watchful editors – words like *infovore, firescape, cli-fi, fanfic, showrooming* and *onesie.*

The high-tech way is to get the computer to do the work of collecting and analysing texts. Data is plentiful these days and a spellchecker is the ultimate if rather crude means of identifying words not in the dictionary.

Finally we rely on contributors, these days mostly contributors from our website. A new word here, a meaning there, a definition that could be worded a little better. All offered in a spirit of helpfulness and prompted by a shared interest in Australian English and a love of language.

The wisdom of Humpty Dumpty

There are two common opposing points of view about language – one, that we arrive at the meanings that we give our words by a process of convention and two, that a word has a 'right meaning' and that departures from this are a sign of decay.

There is a third point of view on all this that is put forward by Humpty Dumpty in *Through the Looking Glass,* the sequel to *Alice's Adventures in Wonderland* by Lewis Carroll. He proposes a kind of linguistic anarchy in which we each have the right to make words mean whatever we want them to mean:

> 'When I use a word…it means what I choose it to mean – neither more nor less.'
>
> 'The question is,' said Alice, 'whether you can make words mean so many different things.'
>
> 'The question is,' said Humpty Dumpty, 'which is to be master – that's all.'

Creative writers tend to subscribe to the Humpty Dumpty view. Their skill lies in putting a new spin on a word so that its meaning is subtly altered. Uniqueness of meaning is what they labour to achieve.

Humpty Dumpty had used the word *glory* to mean 'a nice knock-down argument' and dismissed Alice's protests as the petulant talk of an ignorant child. Writers do not on the whole treat the language with the arrogance of Humpty Dumpty, but they are focused on what their creativity can achieve rather than on the substance of the language that we all share. If you regard Australian English as a house in which we all live, writers are creating stunning effects on the walls on which they place their individual mark, but are only dimly aware that the structure is something that is communally owned.

A long time ago now David Ireland was writer-in-residence at Macquarie University and as such was invited to visit the dictionary. Since we had him at the lunch table we thought we would ask him about a few interesting usages we had found in his writing. These were not part of his style as a writer but just ordinary words used in a slightly less than ordinary way.

In this case I felt that the author was not just surprised but taken aback. Despite all our assurances that we were not calling him to account for this but just trying to work out whether he felt that his usage was mainstream or slightly odd, he behaved rather like a motorist who has just been dished out a traffic infringement on a law that he didn't know existed. Writers spend so much of their lives avoiding hackneyed use that they cease to appreciate the conventional in language.

I have found this to be a common reaction – writers draw their words under their wings like outraged chooks until that nasty dictionary person goes away and it is safe for the little darlings to come out into the sunshine of literary creativity.

The exception to this is David Malouf who is not only superbly original as a writer but has an awareness of the variety of English within which he writes and has his being. As David said:

Insofar as we are a people here, and insomuch as we have a culture, it is absolutely rooted in that language [Australian English]. That language is what holds us together. You know when people are always looking around for what defines the Australian identity, or defines us as a community, or a nation or whatever it is, it seems to me to reside less in particular

> *characteristics than in the fact that we share that*
> *language with one another and have changed that*
> *language in ways that fit us …*

This is the house we share.

The decline of the hyphen

The first thing to say about hyphens is that there are a lot fewer of them than there used to be. In general over the past few decades we have tossed out buckets of commas, hyphens, dashes and so on, on the basis that the text reads quite well without them. Punctuation has always been a matter of actual need tempered by fashion so there is scope for quite a lot of variation in the treatment of texts with a tension between community expectations and individual taste.

The question of hyphens in compound nouns – the presence or absence – causes some people a problem because there seems to be no logic to it. What line are we to take with *canegrowers*, *wheat growers* and *fruit-growers*, and can that line be sustained with *oyster growers* – is that *oyster-growers* or *oystergrowers*?

If *canegrower* and *canecutter* are both one word, why does *cane sugar* seem to resist any efforts to bring its elements together?

There is an underlying process that influences these outcomes. Most compounds start out in life as two words that become fused in our minds, then in print, as the compound gains currency and we cease to analyse it into its component parts. An intermediate stage is often the hyphenated variant, which usually reflects our moment of wavering before we commit ourselves to the noun as a unit and the two words are set solid.

Sometimes this can happen very quickly. Take the case of *email*, which began with a hyphenated prefix *e-* standing for *electronic*. For a while we read this new word as *electronic mail*, but familiarity dispenses with etymology and we accepted *email* for what it was and dropped the hyphen. The word *online* is another one that went through this process in the computer explosion of new words.

Nevertheless, there are factors that can act against this fusion of words, factors such as awkwardness in spelling. There are some of us who are still not happy to spell *co-operate* without a hyphen because we are irritated by the presence of *coop* at the beginning of the word. Another difficulty is that the resulting compound is too long to be analysed quickly. *Cabinet-maker* may well keep the hyphen because *cabinetmaker* is visually indigestible. Others resist fusion for inexplicable reasons. A *canecocky* may be one word but a *cow cocky* stubbornly insists on being two.

What ought to be sets of words appearing in the dictionary and treated in the same way, can present an alarming amount of variation. Look at the entries for *bush* and its compounds in the *Macquarie*, and the rhyme, that is to say, the language intuitions may be there, but not the reason. The rules might be general but the application is on a word-by-word basis.

The final complication is that all language is in a state of flux so what you see as two words today might well be hyphenated tomorrow and set solid the day after that. The result is an editor's nightmare, if that editor has the kind of mind that likes to group words in orderly sets and sit them up straight at the lexical table.

For the reader, the situation that arises in the dictionary where you can compare all the different compounds of *bush* is most unusual. Words may be drawn together in sets in the dictionary by the power of alphabetical order but in real life they are encountered one by one in different contexts so that one is rarely affronted by the variation among them.

If by chance these words line up together in a fashion that is distracting to the reader, then it falls to the editor, as always, to find the decent way out. The dictionary tries to present the general form of the word but usually other variants are listed, so it is always possible to choose the variant form that causes the least distress in a difficult situation.

Australians – a hypocoristic lot

Hypocoristic forms are the affectionate diminutives that are common in Australian English – words like *ambo* for 'ambulance officer', *cuie* for 'cucumber' and *rellies* for 'the relatives'. *Macquarie Dictionary* comments that *-ie* can be used as a sign of affection (*kiddies*), a familiar abbreviation (*postie* or *pressie*), or as a functional way of turning an adjective into a noun (*greenie*, *littlie*). The word *hypocorism* is from the Greek *hypo*, meaning 'somewhat', and *koros*, meaning 'child'.

The suffix *-o* on the other hand probably began with the cries of street vendors who found that adding *-o* to the end of the commodity they were selling gave them something that would help carry the voice. Thus we have *milko* and *rabbitoh*. Other occupations and pursuits are treated in a similar manner (*garbo*, *journo*) and from this we reach the point where any kind of distinctive feature can be turned into a noun by an efficient technique for stereotyping, as in *derro*, *plonko*.

In many instances *-ie* and *-o* serve the same purpose. Why *arvo* and not *arvie*, *demo* and not *demie*. Indeed *commo* and *commie* are weakly interchangeable. A sense of language rhythm dictates which option works best in what circumstances.

Impact

The starting point here is the phrasal verb *to impact on* meaning 'to have a strong effect on' as in *This impacts on me badly*. From here we have slipped into a transitive verb with the same meaning as in *This impacts me badly*. This usage can seem odd, even irritating, to those who have not grown up with it, but it has great currency and it is not likely to go away. I suppose it has the appeal of simplicity. You can use it in the active (*misfortune impacted him badly*) or the passive (*he was badly impacted by misfortune*) without finding a stray particle on your hands that forces you to rethink the sentence. It has the same meaning as *affect* but, at least when it first became a buzzword, it did have more clout. It has perhaps been overused now so that it is no longer striking but, for the reasons given above, it is still useful.

Internet gibberish

Beware the purveyor of cheap thrills who tells you that the internet will be the end of the English language as we know it, that a horrible gibberish is about to overwhelm standards of writing and that, even worse, we can abandon correct spelling because it doesn't matter anymore.

I attended a conference recently where one of the participants applied a computer parsing program to the text of a chat room and came up, not surprisingly, with a number of horrendous errors. The parser appeared to have suffered a nervous breakdown when confronted by this fundamentally different language and had to be put on a diet of concrete nouns to restore its sanity.

The parser was geared for standard mainstream text far removed from the style, content and intentions of the chat room. It had no idea what to do with emoticons, those little symbols devised by using the possibilities of the keyboard. For happiness read :), :(for sadness. Or with the range of new abbreviations that are developing – *lol* for 'laugh out loud' or

P for 'putting my tongue out' or *u* for 'you'. The other disturbing thing was the breakdown of the relationships between strands of text. In a chat room lines of conversation do not necessarily follow each other as they would in the stagy dialogue of novels. They are closer to what happens in normal conversation where sentences peter out, interrupt each other, where sometimes there are two conversations going at once, the participants in each particular exchange hearing selectively through the noise. In the chat room threads of conversation interweave so that it is quite normal for a participant to respond to a line further back as if nothing had come between.

This is not like any writing we have experienced in the past but this should not disturb us unduly. It is not the first time that a new genre has evolved to meet special circumstances.

The language of the chat room has the immediacy, the ephemerality, the disjointedness of speech, but it lacks the extras of speech – the modulation of voice, the expressive stuff we do with our hands and face as the punctuation of non-verbal communication.

Somehow this conversation-in-text had to capture non-verbal information quickly enough so as not to impede the flow. Long parentheses explaining the participant's mood, attitude and relationship to others will not do. And so emoticons came into being – the quick hint as to frame of mind.

The rhythm of the chat room is slower than that of normal conversation with participants quite happy to drift in and out – sometimes having observer status, sometimes being an active participant. But it all has to be typed. This generation acquires keyboard skills at an early age but even so the pace has to be kept up or the rhythm of the exchanges is destroyed. Thus the need for the many abbreviations.

And as for spelling – the attitude has been that in this fast, fast world, who cares about the occasional typo? It's just a case of the mind travelling at the speed of light and the fingertips at something regrettably less than that. It has almost become a badge of pride. In cyberspace the race is to the cyberswift – lesser mortals have hang-ups about spelling.

Lately, however, I have taken to checking my email with greater care. I remember that when faxes came in we had to learn as a matter of judgement when to fax and when to retreat to the greater formality and slower pace of the standard letter. In the same way I think that we will sort out where in our digital communications we can adopt a style that includes a degree of informality, and where we need to protect ourselves with a conscious formality and disinclination to abandon the standards of print.

Keeping up with invented words

Every now and then I am reminded how little of the language the dictionary actually captures, how much is going on out there that is ephemeral, individual, eccentric and funny. The dictionary has, until the coming of online lexicography, been constrained by its ration of pages, and so rules have been developed for what is a 'real' word and what is not. Family inventions, for example, are not 'real' words in the eyes of the dictionary, even though a particular family may enjoy them and use them regularly. Similarly there is a wealth of humorous invention, some of which travels quite widely around the world, which is not deemed suitable dictionary material. Thank goodness – I would not like to have to keep up with the likes of *percussive maintenance* – the fine art of whacking a device to get it working, or *beepilepsy* – a condition affecting those with vibrating pagers characterised by sudden spasms, goofy facial expressions and loss of speech. The *ohno-second* – that minuscule fraction of time in which you realise you've just made a big mistake – is a joke I have heard before. Time will tell whether these witticisms have the staying power to make their way into the official record of the language.

Language and culture

Varieties of English are distinguished largely by accent and lexicon, the latter containing items that are wrought from the experience of the language community. This experience often begins at the material level – in Australia, for example, with *bush*. In India we might select *jungle* and in Asia *rice bowl*. From these facts of our existence we then weave a web of metaphor. In Australian English we move from *bush* as an adjective meaning 'found or made or operating in the bush' to *bush* meaning 'crude or improvised', and this is productive of lexical items like *bush lawyer* and *bush cure*. Similarly in Indian English *jungle* has the sense of 'rough-and-ready' leading to the term *jungle raj* as in 'Are we living in a jungle raj or a democracy?' In English in Asia the *rice bowl* is a metaphor for the means of earning a living, as in 'daily rice-bowl issues that worry the voters'. In China *iron rice bowl* became the term for a government job from which it was pretty well impossible to be sacked, which allows a playful extension of the metaphor as in *The smashing of the iron rice bowl is putting millions out of work even as it improves the income of those still at work.*

Apart from the shift from the literal to the metaphorical, such key terms, because of their significance to the culture, tend to form numerous compounds that develop into collocational clusters, which vary from one variety to another. For example, in Australian English a key term like *bush* produces pages in the dictionary devoted to its compounds. Similarly in English in Asia *bamboo* is a key term producing such compounds as *bamboo chair, bamboo curtain* (the literal one), *bamboo fan, bamboo flute, bamboo paper, bamboo salt, bamboo slice* (for writing on), *bamboo toothpaste*, and *silk and bamboo genre* (a romantic style of popular novel in Asia). Similarly *dragon* produces a range of such items including the expression *jump the dragon gate*, which is a reference to a folk story about koi jumping upstream until they make the final jump and become dragons. In Chinese English this comes to mean 'to overcome all difficulties and obstacles'. In this way a variety of English is a vehicle, just as much as a language other than English, for reflecting the culture of the community that shapes it.

The *Macquarie Atlas of Indigenous Australia* has one map that lingers in my mind. It shows different themes linked to the words used as the name for a policeman. Confronted with this new type of being, different tribes extended the meaning of different words of their language to encompass 'policeman'. The words whose meanings were extended in this way were linked to such concepts as anger, black clothing, fierce bird, taboo, stone (possibly a reference to money), poison or bitter tasting things and rope for tying. They make a menacing set.

Language jokes

There's many a word that starts out in jest and ends up being taken in dreadful seriousness. My father always used to say 'Peace, perturbed spirit' when my mother was beseeching, entreating, scolding, nagging him to do something. I always thought it was a phrase he had made up until I recognised the original in the ghost scene in *Hamlet* and burst out laughing. The class was puzzled and I had a few mumbled explanations to make to the teacher.

The same problem has arisen with *obstropolous* – another word that my father used, but which I somehow twigged was a joke word for *obstreperous*. *Obstropolous children* sound so much worse than *obstreperous* ones. But not all of us, particularly when we first hear these words as children, realise that there is a joke attached to their use. In a child's accepting way we assume that this is a real word, solid and acceptable, that we are encountering. That assumption can stay with us for life – or at least until someone points out to us the error of our ways. I had a letter from a school principal who had used *obstropolous* all his life, no doubt to children who richly deserved it, and who had in retirement caught up with the word *obstreperous* whose existence he had never suspected.

The *obstropolous* joke is of long standing. It goes back in British English to the disdain with which speakers of standard British English regarded speakers of dialect. You can see the caption in *Punch* – British Bobby: 'But Your Honour, he was a-being werry obstropolous'. This joke against the ignorant became a cliché. In Australia it is hard to know what its path might have been. Was it a dialectal hand-me-down that had increased currency in mainstream Australian English? Or was it the remnant of a joke that lingered on in the language awareness of the community? The word remaining long after the context of the joke had been forgotten.

'Beresque' for *berserk* is a more recent joke but has proved popular, while 'sparrow grass' for *asparagus* is a variation brought out to amuse the children, possibly because it seems easier to say, possibly because it makes the meal more palatable.

There are other blemishes on our English that result from just getting it wrong the first time. We seem to set a groove in a grey cell that is hard to eradicate. The person who owns up to saying 'mischievious' for *mischievous* realises that he has said it for longer than he cares to remember. Who among us can cast the first stone?

As far as the joke words go, I remember my mother's admonition to my father before some great occasion – 'Please, dear, don't tell any jokes. People will only misunderstand you'.

Language scapes

In various parks and lookouts around the country we are given the opportunity to measure our present existence against our past. Look, we say, there is a large building where there was once a hut. A container terminal where there used to be a jetty. A hill where now there is a level plain.

We measure ourselves in language in much the same way. The various editions of the dictionary are the monuments that map the language terrain. By comparing one edition with another we can see what has shifted in our environment and culture.

As we survey the language scene we can observe that there are the solid edifices of science (*gravity well*), health (*deep vein thrombosis*), computers (*domain name system*), and law (*mandatory sentencing*) – these are lexical structures that are here to stay.

But computers also give us *mummy blog* and *digerati* – these are like the gaily coloured awnings set around the building that may fade over the years and be replaced.

Then there are the hastily erected temporary structures – the here-today-and-gone-tomorrow of colloquialism. Such terms as *eye candy, hissy fit, mojo* and *brainiac* may have a short-term life – they are intended to be demolished and replaced freely.

There are probably more of these temporary buildings than there are permanent structures since fashion affects many aspects of our lives – food (*gravlax, bento box, friand*); fashion (*cargo pants, body art, pashmina*); popular music (*dance music, boy/girl band*); film and TV (*chick flick, reality TV, lifestyle show*).

There's the opportunity, too, for a bit of local design with items like *chook chaser, do the Harry, pub band* and *muffin top*.

Think back to the first edition, which included such features as *chequebook journalism, boat people, buzzword, legionnaire's disease, reggae, bio engineering* and *CAT scan*.

Compare this with the latest edition of the dictionary with such items as *dining boom, fanfic, facepalm, coffee cupping, firescape, onesie, marriage equality, generation debt* and *dumb phone*.

Each edition of the dictionary reveals how the world has changed.

Language snobbery
still lives

Who would have thought that Julia Gillard's accent would have caused such a fuss? Even Labor supporters who agreed with everything Julia said apparently had great difficulty coping with the way in which she said it. One blogger found it easier to believe that Julia had fabricated her accent and was bunging it on to score brownie points with the traditional Labor voters than to believe that a lawyer 'could sound like that'. Despite others declaring that many an educated Adelaidian from 'the working class' would sound exactly like Julia, this cynic could not be persuaded.

Possibly the fact that Gillard was a woman went against her as well. In Australian society, men who have spoken with broad accents have been accepted as honest and genuine though perhaps not clever. Many Australian males have the ability to adjust their accent according to their circumstances so that they can be one of the blokes or a cut above the blokes, depending on what is needed. But women have always been encouraged to be and sound refined (that is, 're-fained') and so their accent has generally moved away from broad and towards genteel. A woman flaunting a broad accent is an affront.

There were those online who argued that, whether you liked it or disliked it, Gillard's accent sounded authentic. It reminded me of the comment of a correspondent to *The Daily Telegraph* (Sydney), 22 December 1926:

> *An Australian accent is as essential to Australian patriotism as an Australian flag. It matters little whether it be a twang or a brogue or a bleat, so long as it is real. And to be real it must be a spontaneous production of the Australian environment.*
> *Everything else is shoddy.*

I thought that, these days, all accents were accepted as part of a person's life baggage, sometimes telling you something about their background but often nothing that mattered very much as to their future. I thought that Dame Edna had mocked this sort of re-fain-ment to the point where we had laughed it out of our systems. It seems so old-fashioned to be so hung up about a particular accent. For some of us, however, Gillard was on the wrong side of the white picket fence the minute she opened her mouth.

Larrikin

The larrikin of the late 1800s in colonial Australia was not a pleasant fellow – robbery, rape, murder were part of his life. Thug, bully, member of a street gang – these are the definitions. However, as Louis Stone remarks in *Jonah* (1911), larrikins were remarkably neat in their appearance. They favoured tight-fitting bell-bottomed dark suits with a lot of buttons, soft white shirts with new black mufflers around their necks in place of collars and soft black felt hats. Their shoes were noteworthy, tight fitting with narrow high heels and lots of brass eyelets on the uppers. The term *larrikin* seems to have been inherited from British dialect where it referred to a flashily dressed young man. A popular story tells of an Irish policeman giving evidence in a Melbourne court in 1869, whose pronunciation of *larking* was more like *larriking*, but after diligent searching no one can find any record of such a case. However, it is still possible that the origin of the word is in the Yorkshire *larack about*, which is a variant of *lark about*.

Licence and license

The pair *licence* and *license* are often confused.

Licence is the noun and *license* is the verb.

You can remember this by lining them up beside the much simpler case of *advice/advise* where the pronunciations are different and so there is no confusion. The word with the *-ce* ending is the noun. The word with the *-se* ending is the verb.

If we look at the etymology of the word we go back through French to Latin. In French and other Romance languages the spelling is with *-c-*, drawn from the French *licence* from the Latin *licentia* meaning 'permission'. In English, therefore, both noun and verb ought to be spelled with a *-c-*.

But in English *advice* and *advise* (which have separate etymological paths) had already set up the idea of a rule where the noun took *-c-* and the verb took *-s-*, and so *practice/practise* and *prophecy/prophesy* followed. And so it seemed clear that *licence/license* should go down that path too.

The Americans then confused the issue by deciding that they would opt for *-s-* in both noun and verb as being a simpler solution. This, by the way, was the choice of Dr Johnson in his dictionary.

We struggle on with one spelling for the noun and the other for the verb.

Good luck with it!

Linguicism

Deciding who should go first through a revolving door is one of the small crises of etiquette. A larger and newer difficulty is deciding who should speak in what language when the social situation presents options.

In my spare time I play keyboard for a small music group dominated by South Americans. Rehearsals were on for a big performance which, in Latin style, is never thought to be complete without food and dancing, so the big discussion on the empanadas was under way – how many to make and how to get them there.

Keyboard players are noticed when they make a mistake but apart from that they tend to fade into the background, so having packed my gear away I sat down and listened to the discussion (incomprehensible to me) that was going on in Spanish. It seemed to me perfectly natural that it should be in Spanish given that it concerned the Spanish speakers in the group who wanted to go into a level of detail and culinary concern that their English would not allow. When it came to empanadas, the keyboard player had nothing to contribute.

But one of the speakers noticed my presence and immediately apologised for having overridden my English with their Spanish. The apology was dignified but firm – it was unthinkable that the group could proceed in anything but English since I was there.

I pondered this question of language etiquette and decided that I still felt it perfectly reasonable and perfectly polite for the group to have finished this particular discussion in Spanish. Perhaps the decision to speak English was born of long experience as a speaker of what is in this country a minority language, which leads to excessive pandering to the Englishness of the mainstream.

I am sure it is difficult for speakers of minority languages to retain the right perspective on this. Even without any intentional negativity the mainstream language, by sheer weight of numbers and omnipresence, has a stifling effect.

In some situations this is made worse by actual hostility, which emanates from that insidious desire we all have to be like each other. It starts in childhood where of course it is an essential part of development, leading a bunch of rugged infantile individualists to be caring, sharing and communal human beings. But retained in adulthood, this antipathy to difference can produce frightening results.

Do we oppress minority languages because we are frightened by such an obvious form of difference? The word for this reaction is linguicism – another '-ism' to put beside racism, ageism, etc.

Of course not all of us react that way – some people embrace the new, relish the variety of experience and regard sitting in a cafe without being able to understand a word of what is being said at the next table as one of those mind-openers to be valued.

Even such open-minded people can be conditioned into giving other languages less than their due by the conventions of the moment. The rules about who speaks what language when are rules of etiquette. That is to say they are merely conventional, merely the accepted practice, the 'way we do it in this country'. We therefore need to be on the lookout for underlying linguicism disguised as good manners.

In my particular case I accepted the gracious gesture of the change to English but my lasting feeling was that I should have given the empanada group a bit of consciousness-raising. Not all communications have to take place in English just because there is an English speaker present. Especially not communications about empanadas, which I am pleased to say survived the English turn of the conversation and were absolutely delicious.

Do I mean literally?

The problem with *literally* is that the world seems to be losing its sense of humour. *Literally* is supposed to work as a marker indicating that an expression used figuratively should be read in its absolute literal meaning. This twist is sometimes quite witty because you can read the expression both ways – in its literal and figurative meaning. For example, according to ABC News, Mr Mal Brough remarked that the then NSW Premier Bob Carr asked for an extension 'literally at the 11th hour – one minute to midnight'. So we read 'at the 11th hour' to mean very, very late in the process. But no – we read further. The letter arrived within that 11th hour – at one minute to midnight. So both the literal and the idiomatic use of the phrase are true.

There are two kinds of mistakes in the use of *literally*. The first is just boring. It is the use of *literally* with a phrase that has no figurative or idiomatic meaning and would have been taken at face value anyway. For example, a very rare 'painted lady' opal was put on show for only the second time since it was discovered.

The manager of the museum where it was to be displayed commented that since the first viewing 'it has literally been in the opal miner's cellar'. Well, there is no great play on words there. To be 'in the cellar' is not a collocation or idiom that has special significance. The fact of the matter is that the opal has been in the miner's cellar – end of story.

The second error is the use of *literally* to add emphasis to an idiom which, while perfectly acceptable in its figurative meaning, ought to give rise to a certain amount of laughter if taken in its literal meaning. For example, former Senator Amanda Vanstone, in anticipation of a meeting with backbenchers to discuss immigration changes, commented that 'we are literally bending over backwards to take into account concerns raised by colleagues'. The thought of Vanstone and her department all bending over backwards should make us smile.

But increasingly *literally* is used to add emphasis, without a flicker of amusement in the minds of either speakers or listeners at the image that is conjured up. Where has their sense of humour gone?

Should *man boobs* be in the dictionary?

This was the question put to me by one interviewer who obviously still subscribed to the view that some words were proper, and some not. *Westie* also troubled him as being 'ungrammatical'. It is odd how this somewhat biblical view of the dictionary survives. Sheep over here lined up neatly from A to Z and leatherbound with gold foil. Goats over there in the scruffy paperback with hideous jokes and devilish designs on the front cover. When in fact the dictionary takes them all, sheep and goats, with tags attached of course, but in every other respect given equal status within the neutral framework of alphabetisation. The term *man boobs* is one we would regard as a colloquialism although there is no formal equivalent. It is difficult to imagine an archbishop using it in a sermon, which is one test of informality. Similarly, a *westie* is not just a person from the west, but a particular stereotype of the western suburbs of Sydney. There is no formal equivalent. We accept that the dictionary gives us the full account of the language from taboo items to its loftiest and most arcane terms. But *man boobs* goes one step further. It makes us laugh, and the dictionary, as we all know, is the most serious of reference books. Perhaps that is what caused the problem.

Maroon

Each year as we approach the Rugby League State of Origin series, we pause again to consider that oddity of Australian English – the pronunciation of *maroon* to rhyme with *bone*. Statistics show that about two thirds of us rhyme *maroon* with *bone* while the other third rhyme it with *moon*. The British and the Americans go the *moon* path. It is not known where we got our preferred pronunciation since the one to rhyme with *moon* would seem to be the most obvious choice. There is a suggestion that it is slightly closer to the Italian *marrone* meaning 'chestnut', which is its origin (via French). More convincingly there is some evidence to say that this is a case of hypercorrection propped up by various teachers and gentrified parents who have insisted that this is the 'proper' pronunciation, and who are wary of the pronunciation rhyming with *moon* because it seems too much like a spelling pronunciation, and therefore has to be wrong!

Mate

While *mate* is a word that goes back a long way in British English, it has a special place in Australian English. Ultimately it is of Germanic origin and refers to the person with whom you share your food.

In the 1800s in Australia, a mate was a person who worked with you in the bush where life was tough and sometimes dangerous for a man travelling alone. Mates were partners in enterprises like shearing and mining and shared their earnings. The word had a solid meaning then which was coloured by emotion when the mates went to war. But meaning leached out through the 1900s until we get to a citation from 1972: 'A mate in Australia is simply that which a bloke must have around him. Mates do not necessarily want to know you'. Finally we come to its use as a form of greeting between men, as exemplified in a conversation between business-man Nick Whitlam and Malcolm Turnbull in 1990, as reported in *The Sydney Morning Herald*: 'His last words as Whitlam walked out of the door concluded with that most ominous of political salutations. It ended in "mate" is all Whitlam can remember'.

There is a postscript to the story of *mate*. With the arrival of feminism in Australia, women took to calling each other 'mate'. There is a certain bravado and stylishness in this, but also, I think, a sense that mateship *is* an important thing in Australian culture and that women ought not to be excluded from it.

When we don't all mean the same thing

In our dealings with a Chinese printer on one edition of the dictionary we struck a snag in the form of the entry for Taiwan, the point at which politics and lexicography had to establish a definition compatible to both. The problem was how to find a wording for a situation that is clearly defined by China on the one hand, has a different definition within Taiwan and is being maintained as a political ambiguity by everyone else.

Taiwan as a geographical entity was accepted as long as it was made plain that we were talking about the island of Taiwan, not the political entity of Taiwan. So in dealing with plants and animals we used a formula that made a distinction between the mainland of China and the island of Taiwan. We then had to consider the treatment of people – politicians, artists, writers, filmmakers. Were they Taiwanese or Chinese? Normally the dictionary would not go to a state or provincial level in its description. Peter Sculthorpe is an Australian composer, not a Tasmanian composer or even a Tasmanian-born composer. But do you do an injustice to Ang Lee who always describes himself as a Taiwanese-born filmmaker to enter him in the dictionary as Chinese? We considered whether we were being fair to describe Tiananmen as the site of a massacre when the Kent State University massacre was not even given an entry. But in the end none of it mattered. In a climate of political tension, the printer, whose licence was on the line if someone took offence, decided that tactful formulas were not good enough. A guarantee from the government against prosecution was the only truly safe assurance. Sadly, we had to find another printer.

Did she mince her words?

Former prime minister Julia Gillard ruffled some parliamentary feathers with her contrasting of parliamentary styles as macho versus mincing, the Doberman versus the poodle. As dictionary editor, I was called on to give some background on the word *mincing*. The first part was easy. *Mincing* is from an Old French word meaning 'to make small' and came to be used to describe young ladies with coy and excessively demure manners. However it is fair to say that any search on Google will reveal that a mincing walk, along with a limp wrist, is part of the stereotypical description of a particular kind of gay man. Ms Gillard did not refer to mincing walks but to a mincing performance style. The leap from her choice of adjective to gay labelling is there for those who wish to take it, but she was not selling tickets at the departure point.

One good thing that came out of it was that it provoked a string of Keating reminiscences. The time that he said that John Howard was 'a shiver looking for a spine to crawl up'. Or that Malcolm Fraser looked like 'an Easter Island statue with an arse full of razor blades'. Keating wasn't one to mince his words.

Mind your p's and q's

Sometimes the most familiar expressions have the haziest origins. One such is *mind your p's and q's* where theories abound but evidence is wanting. The phrase possibly derives from the common tendency of children learning to write to confuse *p* and *q* because you have to remember on which side the downward stroke belongs. Another suggestion is that it comes from the practice in English public houses of the 19th century to serve ale in either pints or quarts, with Ps or Qs, the letter abbreviations being chalked up on a board as a tally. Obviously it was a matter of some concern to the drinkers that the landlord was careful. Alternatively the concern was theirs because if they lost track they would find themselves short of money when the reckoning came around.

The only thing I can say for sure is that in the earliest citations going back to the 1790s the meaning is 'make sure you are very correct in your behaviour'. The first citation is from a woman and her tone is genteel, so this is a drawing room expression rather than a collo-quialism. If the original context had been the pub you would expect the meaning to be 'make sure you are accurate and honest in your dealings' and the flavour of the phrase to be more colloquial. A bloke's expression, you might say.

But as I say, no one really knows.

Misogyny

Who would have thought that the entry on *misogyny* would have pulled *Macquarie Dictionary* into such a media storm? The word entered the English language in the 1600s as the anglicised version of the Greek word and pottered along with infrequent use until the 1890s where it was taken up in psychology and given a partner in *misandry*. Somewhere in the 1900s, but increasingly in the feminist discourse of the latter part of the century, it became a synonym for 'sexism', both words referring to a general prejudice against women as opposed to an individual's pathological mental state. The first meaning of the word, 'hatred of women', still stands as a definition in the dictionary. So much confusion was caused by the notion that this meaning was being replaced by the one relating to prejudice.

The notion of a conspiracy here – that the dictionary was in cahoots somehow with the PM of the day – is highly amusing. It would be fun to be a *lexicographe grise* but the probability that I would find such a role in politics is not high. Back to my drudgery.

In this instance the whole discussion kicked off with a phone call to the dictionary from a journalist at the *Financial Review* who was prompted by the debate about the meaning of the word to ask the editors of the dictionary what we thought.

Also amusing to watch were the virtuous pedants-in-politics, clutching their *Oxford Concise* dictionaries of about 30 years ago, and maintaining that the *Oxford English Dictionary* would never do such a thing. Just to rub salt into the wound they scoffed that *Macquarie* was the sort of dictionary that would allow *decimate* to mean 'annihilate'. Of course the most recent and comprehensive edition of the OED allows both these changes in meaning. The editor of the OED, John Simpson, enjoyed the opportunity to have a dig at *Macquarie* for being so behind the times – he had expanded the meaning of *misogyny* in 2002.

Subtle changes in the use of a word can fly under the radar for some time, often until there is some kind of discourse, public or otherwise, which brings them to the attention of the dictionary editors. Like everyone else, we watch TV, listen to the radio, read the newspaper. I even read all the advertising material stuffed into the letterbox because it is a good guide to fashions in food and clothing and appliances.

The entries for *misogyny* and *misandry* each have two definitions, one covering hatred and the other covering prejudice. They possibly need a usage note to acknowledge their moment in Australian politics, when the dictionary's standard comment of 'some people will object to this change' generated particular heat.

What moment are you having?

Some words give us scope to play and become what linguists would term 'productive'. *Moment* is one such word. It seems to have taken a leap forward in the expression *a senior moment*, that temporary forgetfulness associated with the ageing process, but has now added a *blonde moment* to its repertoire. The reference to the stereotype of the ditzy blonde can usefully capture that moment of extreme stupidity that we wish to explain away. This leads to the question – how many other kinds of moments are we having? We will hope for more creativity in this direction.

My Lady Mondegreen

A mondegreen is 'a word or phrase which results from a mishearing or misinterpretation of the original words, especially in song lyrics, as *Australians all eat ostriches* instead of *Australians all let us rejoice*, the first line of the national anthem'. (*Macquarie Dictionary*)

It comes from a mistake of that kind made by an American writer, Sylvia Wright, who reminisced about the way her mother used to read aloud to her when she was a child. A favourite was a poem from *Percy's Reliques*, which began (or so she thought): 'Ye Highlands and ye Lowlands, Oh, where hae ye been? They hae slain the Earl Amurray, And Lady Mondegreen'. The correct version was 'They have slain the Earl O' Murray And they laid him on the green'. Wright coined the word *mondegreen* from this experience and it caught on.

A full mondegreen version of the Australian national anthem is:

Australians all eat ostriches
Four minus one is three.
With olden royals, we're fair and loyal,
Our home is dirt by sea.
I learned to bounce on nature strips
In booties stitched with care.
In mystery's haze, let's harvest maize
And plant azaleas there.
Enjoy full trains and let us in
And dance Australia yeah!

Anon.

The difference between
a nationalist and
a patriot

We became accustomed, eventually, to biting one-liners from Paul Keating, but one of his media appearances gave me food for thought. Keating claimed that John Howard was a nationalist (putting him, in the process, in the same camp – or should that be Kampf? – as Adolf Hitler) but not a patriot on the grounds that:

> *a patriot will not exclude a person from another race from the community where they have lived side by side and whom he has known for many years but a nationalist will always remain suspicious of someone who does not seem to belong to his kind of people or more likely his kind of thinking.*

So what does the dictionary say about the meanings of these two words? The entry for *nationalism* in the *Macquarie Dictionary* covers a range of different aspects. It begins with the simple idea of 'national spirit or aspirations', then colours that with the notion of finding independence, protecting the interests of one's country (often to the detriment of everyone else's interests) and ends up with excessive zeal and devotion to one's own country. The notion of *patriotism* is much less complicated – simple devotion to one's country.

I looked at corpus evidence for these two words and it seemed to me that there is a difference that perhaps the dictionary does not quite capture. *Patriotism* is strongly linked to demonstrations of this devotion – flags and national anthems and the like – and the notion of the ultimate sacrifice of going to war and dying for one's country. The worst that could be said about patriotism is that is can be misguided (*blind patriotism* is not desirable) or debased and sentimentalised.

The evidence for the use of *nationalism* took me into murkier waters and into a split between the experience of nationalism in Australia and elsewhere in the world that is rightly reflected in the multiple definitions in the dictionary. Think 'nationalism' in Europe and you do think of the terrible unfolding of its dark power in World War II. Think 'nationalism' in Australia and you tend to think of our 20th-century endless search for a national identity and separation from Britain.

Nationalism is still for us defined by the Ashes series. We are aware that nationalism can be taken too far – chauvinistic nationalism, jingoism, xenophobia are the signs of a nationalism that has turned bad.

In Australia, nationalism is linked with a shared ethos, a shared culture, a shared way of life. And this is where Keating's analysis came into play, that Howard was claiming the culture that Australia had pre-multiculturalism as the rock on which his nationalism rested and that, in maintaining that culture in the face of the obvious shifts in the shared way of life that Australians have today, he was excluding a number of Australian citizens.

These are powerful words – *nationalism* and *patriotism* – with base meanings that are constantly being coloured by experience. Keating left me pondering whether there is an onus on the dictionary to revisit words of this kind to try to capture more of their nuances.

OK

There are many stories offered about the origin of 'OK'.

First is that it was used as a slogan for the Old Kinderhook Club, a Democratic club of New York of the 1840s. The club was founded by President Martin Van Buren who was born in the village of Kinderhook, New York, and was nicknamed 'Old Kinderhook'.

Yet another suggestion is that Andrew Jackson, in the days before he became President of the United States, borrowed it from the Choctaw Indians, who ended all statements with the phrase *si Hoka* meaning 'that's me' or 'that's what I said'.

Some argued that it was telegraphese, where it stood for 'open key'. The opening of a particular key on the telegraph was a signal that the receiving station was ready for a message to be sent. And, finally, there is the theory that it was borrowed by white America from black America, and that there are a number of West African languages that have such an expression – *o-kay* or *or-kaym* or *eeyi kay* meaning 'yes'.

Evidence has emerged to show that the fashionable and jokey colloquialism, *orl korrect*, current in the 1830s in America, was abbreviated to the even trendier *OK*.

Oops – we all make the odd spelling error

The media are often called to account, not just for pronunciations that fall short of a notional standard but for incorrect grammar and poor spelling. All too often the media is castigated for its slovenly language, but can this be true? Can writers whose skill at capturing information in a readable fashion day in and day out really be guilty of such incompetence?

On the contrary, those who write for the media are usually people who have worked hard at their craft. They often reveal that they are finely attuned to shifts and changes in language and can be held responsible for amplifying a new usage or pronunciation to the broader community. Perhaps what has changed is the culture of the newspapers. Imagine the uproar that once would have followed the misspelling of *millionaire* as it appeared on page 1 of *The Sydney Morning Herald* recently. It was spelled *milionaire*. The newspapers used to have teams of readers whose job was to prevent such an appalling transgression – I was listening to a couple of them reminisce over the silence of the reading room, the struggle to make sure that no error slipped past them, their sense, when the inevitable happened, that they had let down the paper and the journalists who wrote for it. But the reading rooms are gone. Journalists must go to print with nothing but a flimsy spellchecker as protection from the spelling vulnerability that we all share.

Optimists and pessimists

In language, as in life, there are optimists and pessimists. The optimists revel in the new, the pessimists feel threatened by every addition that takes them further away from the secure ground of their own personal lexicon. On top of this natural inclination one way or the other, our education in language matters is rather like a primitive safety drill – hold the child's finger to a split infinitive until the child screams with pain and believe me, that child will never, never split an infinitive again. This does mean that a common legacy of our schooling is that in later life we tend to react to any rational discussion of the split infinitive with a child's cry of, 'Hurt! Hurt! Hurt!'

This is done in schools for sound and caring reasons – a child who splits an infinitive will never make the grade, never pass the exams, never get a good job, never be regarded as one of the discerning. Better the small hurt in childhood for the brighter future as an adult.

We need to set aside the safety drill mentality to accept some of the basic tenets of modern linguistics. One is that language is self-regulating and that each dialect or variety is as linguistically good as any other. Not as prestigious as any other, maybe, but that is a different issue. You may not like the sounds of a particular dialect and you may object violently to its syntax, but this is a matter of the given social order rather than a ranking as superior or inferior in linguistic terms.

Only dead languages don't change; living ones change all the time. Again the self-regulatory aspect will ultimately sort out what changes are permanent from the ephemeral and frivolous tinkerings of happenstance and fashion. On top of choices made by the language itself we can impose community choices. These sometimes are at odds with the inevitable tide of the language and therefore create a split between those people who do what comes naturally and those who know better. And so we have, for example, those who defend the correct use of *disinterested* and *uninterested*, and those who have taken to using *uninterested* with both meanings.

I would put myself with the first group in this particular case, but I would suggest that the defenders of the grammatical faith should remain temperate. The language changes, and tastes change also. We should be prepared to let go particular battles that are no longer worth winning, to learn when to care and when not to care. Matters of taste are not immutable. Indeed, some of the matters of taste have been decided for no very good reason, the split infinitive being a case in point. God did not hand down a style guide, although presumably such questions would have come to His attention for the first time when He wrote the Ten Commandments on the tablets of stone. What was the house style and did He check the spelling?

So what are the issues in contemporary Australian English? Our history has given us a lingering dichotomy between a British tradition and an American influence, the latter being as strong now as it has ever been. That influence is exerted on the entire English-speaking world so we are not alone in feeling overwhelmed by it.

Language optimists welcome these changes, enjoying the glitter of lexical creativity. The pessimists resist all change from the point where they established their own personal norms with regard to lexicon and usage. We need the discussion between creative chaos and conservative order but we should treat each other's points of view with respect.

Panglish

This is a new name for English as it is spoken and written around the world, but what do people mean when they refer to Panglish? Some see it as a kind of pidgin English associated in popular belief with non-native speakers.

If you look at Singapore, most children begin with a first language or home language that is any of various Chinese, Malay or Indian dialects, although there is a strong pressure to reduce the Chinese dialects to Mandarin only. Almost as soon as they go to pre-school, which is at an early age in Singapore, they learn Singlish (the colloquial version of Singaporean English) and, in the classroom, standard Singaporean English. They are ultimately native speakers of Mandarin and Singaporean English.

So the world is not filling up with pidgin English speakers but rather people who are grounded in their regional dialect of English and who then move to what is described as an unmarked form for international communication. By 'unmarked' what is meant is an English stripped of all the local words and idioms that

173

outsiders won't understand. There is no use employing expressions like *mad as a cut snake* or *flat out like a lizard drinking* in an international forum, although the odd distinctive word or phrase can be used for effect as happened with *Crikey!*

The other aspect of this process that hurts the old-guard native speakers of English is the loss of culture – their culture – that has been embedded in English. Newcomers to English don't recognise references to Shakespeare or the Bible so what kind of impoverished English do they speak? Actually, to get the answer to that question we just have to look carefully at the English that the children speak in Australia, and in England, the home of the one true English. There are very few such references to be found in English as she is spoke by the upcoming generations.

Playfulness

Playfulness in language is a constant shimmer on the surface of communication, rarely captured by lexicographers. Whether it is punning, or rhyming slang, or the blending of words, or the code languages of children, it is usually too subtle and ephemeral to be pinned down on the pages of a dictionary.

Occasionally the productions of such play are popularised and survive as words recognised by the whole community. By then much of their sheen has gone. Indeed the embedded words of blends are often forgotten by the time they reach this stage of acceptance. Who remembers that *blotch* is a blend of *blot* and *botch*, that *squirm* is *skew* plus *worm*, that *boost* is *boom* plus *hoist*?

In the Australian context we have *jackaroo* – *Jack* plus *kangaroo* is at least one possibility for the origin of this word – but not much else. We share with the world such mainstream creations as *cyborg* (*cybernetic* plus *organism*), *faction* (*fact* plus *fiction*), *bodacious* (*bold* plus *audacious*), *himbo* (*him* plus *bimbo*) and *bromance* (*brother* plus *romance*). There is one definite strand of blends that toys with place names – *Calexico* and *Mexicali*, *Oxbridge* and *Centralia*. More recently I have encountered *SydMelberra*. And there is of course *BrisVegas*.

When blends are new we still have a sense of the two original words in their truncated elements. This gives us freedom to move, as it were, and to extend the range of the key element by attaching it to other words. *Chocolate* plus *alcoholic* produced *chocaholic*, but it also produced the freely attaching word part *-aholic* which, at different times, has given us *carbo-holic*, *Lotto-holic*, *pastaholic*, *bookaholic*, *shopaholic* and, of course, *workaholic*.

Lewis Carroll gave a name to this construction – portmanteau word – because 'there are two meanings packed up in one word'. The kind of suitcase he had in mind was one with a hinge in the middle of the back, which allowed it to open into two parts.

As is the way with these creations, some are adopted generally, others live only in the context in which they were created. Carroll wrote his down so we still have access to *slithy*, which didn't catch on, and *chortle*, which did.

What has become clear to me is that Carroll was in a tradition of domestic word play which still lives on. Listeners to a radio program in which word blends were discussed offered examples from their own family lexicons such words as *huggle* (*hug* plus *cuddle*), *nibblings* (*nieces/nephews* plus *siblings*), *dehydrangement* (*dehydrate* plus *flower arrangement*) and *snoffle* (*snort* plus *snuffle*).

It is a humbling experience for the dictionary editor to realise that there are words happening out there to which she will probably never have access. Nor do these words need the imprimatur of the diction-ary because they are deemed words by family consent and are all the more important for having this kind of authority.

It is a reminder that the dictionary is a kind of street map to meaning, with major and minor roads indic-ated according to the size and scope of the dictionary. It serves a very useful purpose in helping us to reach the communications that we intend. But, as the street map does not record the footpaths and private avenues of the community, so too the creativity in the language is not written down in the dictionary.

The language of politics

Elections have an added interest for a lexicographer. Along with the glitter of the roadshows and the political jousting, there are the key words that the spin doctors on both sides feed to the candidates in order to keep them on message, the tags that go on the carefully stage-managed barbecue-stoppers. Then there are the words that are tossed in by accident. *Rolled-gold* is a piece of well-worn Australian slang meaning 'top class', which was given new life by Kevin Rudd in his comments on 'rolled-gold election promises'. The environment was obviously a key factor in the debate in that election and produced the trio – *climate sceptic*, *climate realist* and *climate hysteric*.

I have to thank media commentator Mike Carlton for pointing out *bloviator* to me. Apparently Warren Gamaliel Harding (US President 1921–23) was known for his mangling of the English language. This was not the only aspect of his speechmaking that left something to be desired. HL Mencken, author of *The American Language*, said of Harding:

*He writes the worst English that I have ever
encountered. It reminds me of a string of wet sponges;
it reminds me of tattered washing on the line; it
reminds me of stale bean soup, of college yells, of dogs
barking idiotically through endless nights. It is so bad
that a sort of grandeur creeps into it. It drags itself out
of the dark abysm of pish, and crawls insanely up the
topmost pinnacle of posh. It is rumble and bumble. It
is flap and doodle. It is balder and dash.*

It is perhaps a tribute to Harding that his bad speech-making could inspire such wonderful criticism.

Harding is remembered for his coining – or re-coining since it had first appeared in English in 1857 – of the word *normalcy*. *Normality* was the preferred word, although it has to be said in Harding's defence that *normalcy* has now achieved complete normalcy. Often the way in such language debates. Another word that Harding resurrected and made popular from hazy American beginnings was *bloviator*, coined from *blow* meaning 'to brag' with a pseudo-Latin *-iator* ending. A *bloviator* was someone who spoke pompously and at length, the irony being that Harding himself was a prime example. Post-Harding the word became less fashionable in American English but in the 1990s resurfaced in US political-speak with a slight shift in meaning to someone who attempts to speak knowledgeably about subjects on which they are conspicuously ill-informed. And so it arrives in Australian English.

A short history of political correctness

Popular belief has it that the notion of political correctness (PC) began with Mao Zedong. In the *Little Red Book* he asks, 'Where do correct ideas come from?'

This may be drawing a long bow, but there are two aspects of the Chinese experience that are relevant. One is the use of *correctness* to mean 'in line with what the government wants'. The other is the break with the past, since the only way to maintain correctness is to have nothing to do with that incorrectness known as history.

The first example of the use of the term *political correctness* appears in a document emanating from the American National Organization for Women, whose president commented in 1975 that what they were doing was both 'intellectually and politically correct'; that is to say, in line with feminist philosophy and government policy. This is a straightforward use of the expression before it developed its later twists and perversions.

The meaning of *political correctness* drifted a little as it came to be used in relation to organisations that took stands on various social issues. Rather than meaning 'in line with government policy', it came to mean 'in line with a movement taking a particular stand on a social issue'. The relationship to a program-setter was still there but the group setting the program varied.

Finally, the word acquired its general derogatory overtones when it was used as a weapon against such groups by their opponents, who either didn't like the social change advocated or didn't like it being introduced by upstart groups who were not in the conservative tradition of authority. Sometimes these opponents objected to the break with the past, which was an inevitable consequence of change, and sometimes they objected to what they saw as intellectual thuggery on the part of extremists in the radical groups. That these groups were engineering changes in the language as part of their strategy caused particular anguish.

There were extremists among the radicals. For example, wanting to change *manufacture* (literally, 'making by hand') because it had the sequence of letters 'm-a-n' at the start was carrying things a bit too far. More recently, those who hounded a US government worker out of office because he said that he would have to be 'niggardly' with government funds were equally misguided.

Even *Webster's Dictionary* was caught up in excessive zeal – it included *waitron* in its Third Edition as the neutral word replacing *waiter* or *waitress* and, in so doing, broke a cardinal rule of lexicography: that there must be established evidence of the use of a word before it goes into the dictionary.

But often ridiculous examples of PC or 'polcor' words were made up to mock the groups seeking change. The *challenged* series – *vertically-challenged, follicularly-challenged,* and so on – is a running joke, which can lead to opportunistic improvisation.

The final twist came when the new social policy became an accepted part of government policy. The language of bureaucrats has always been fair game. So often the nature of their job leads them to be pompous, deliberately obscure and obsessively safe. They need to sound important, they can rarely say what they mean and they don't dare offend anybody. The mix of PC jargon and bureaucratese has resulted, therefore, in some unfortunate distortions of the language.

Political spin

Politics adds a certain spice to our vocabulary, particularly around election time. We have fond memories of *incentivation*, which has acquired a patina of age and the nostalgia of a remembered tune. Paul Keating is remembered for what former Malaysian Prime Minister Mahathir Mohamad made of the word *recalcitrant*, and for the particular political spin put on the word *arrogant*. Former Leader of the Opposition Kim Beazley left us with *boondoggle*, an introduction of American polispeak, and former politician Barry Jones offered *cadastre* as the idea for the future. The word was borrowed from French in the early 1800s to mean 'a register of property which would serve as the basis for proportional taxation'. The French use derived from the Roman system – *capitastrum* was the register of the poll tax, *caput* meaning 'head'. In this sense of *cadastre* – a register of all the assets of a country – we were re-borrowing the French word in its modern meaning of a public register of all the real property of a country, and then extending it to cover human resources as well as physical ones. As a concept and a word it does not seem to have survived.

Our most successful election coinage was *barbecue stopper*, modelled on the American *water-cooler topic* but made Aussie. Another coinage with Australian connotations was *sandbagging* – the practice of making a number of election promises to a marginal electorate in the hope of shoring up the vote.

I am reliably informed by poet Les Murray that the people around his hometown Bunya on the mid-north coast of NSW refer to Sydney as 'the feedlot'. It is not meant to be a compliment.

Let us not forget the *Dorothy Dixer*, derived from our awareness of Dorothy Dix, the American agony aunt of the 1940s who was suspected of making up letters to herself so that she could give her best replies. But it was an Aussie coinage.

Were they Prisoners of Mother England?

It is a sad fact that folk etymologies are often more satisfying than the true explanation. Poms were not 'Prisoners of Mother England' however intuitively we respond to the image of them in the convict garb with 'POME' stamped on it. The real origin is not an obvious one. It is the notion that *Pommy* is short for *pomegranate*. That image conjures up the shining red cheeks of the newcomers from England, but the appeal lay as much in the rhyme with *immigrant*. The early 1800s produced the rhyming slang *Jimmy Grant* as the nickname for an immigrant. But by the early 1900s this had been transformed to *pommygrant* or *pommy-granates*. The immigrants were still not amused. Little did they know that *Pommy bastard* and *whingeing Pom* lay ahead of them.

The stereotype was of the incompetent newcomer, the man who put a bridle on a horse but neglected to put the bit in its mouth, so it was clear that initially the terms were used to denigrate the newcomers, and it is also clear that the Jimmy Grants and Pommy Grants didn't take to the label very kindly. Later on in the century the origin was forgotten and the force of the term was softened but, with the increased sensitivity to name-calling of any sort, the label *Pommy* has more recently taken a turn for the worse.

Examples of the use of *Jimmy Grant* don't appear until the 1850s (along with the term *Jimmygration*). *Pommy Grant* doesn't appear until the early 1900s so this slang is well after the convict era. The notion of the shiny red British cheeks is folk etymologising after the fact.

Program and programme

When we think of grovelling and scraping and general sycophantic behaviour, we see in our mind's eye a person going out the door backwards while bowing as deeply as possible without falling over. It is a surprise to see sycophancy expressed in spelling choices. We all have personal preferences but when it comes to government documents, the preferences of the individuals should give way to house style representing the greater good. Trying to second-guess the individual style choices of the prime minister of the day, and adapt government style to those preferences, is a very odd and misguided notion.

The reason for a house style is to remove all the time and energy wasted in thrashing out individual preferences. It also provides a consistency to documents from the government, which is appealingly dignified. Once a house style is established it should be changed only when there is a clear and pressing need. Tinkerers should be banned. It makes for unnecessary trouble.

Somewhere down the line there will be someone who hasn't registered the change and presents the (currently) non-preferred spelling.

In this case we have a choice between *programme*, which older Australians see as British spelling, and *program*, which older Australians see as American spelling. If you look back into the history of the word you find that *program* was the accepted English spelling until the British love of all things French in the 19th century produced the Frenchified spelling, *programme*. The Americans were untroubled by all this and retained the spelling *program*, so they could be said to have the original and most correct spelling of the word (for those who like the argument that what comes first is best).

Then we derived the computer program from America and with it the spelling *program* for all computer-related items. Rather than have two spellings for what is the essentially the same word, some of us switched to *program* for all meanings. There is still a tendency in the Australian community to have concert programmes and computer programs — to allocate one spelling to the arts and the other to IT. Dictionaries give *program* as the first choice and *programme* as a minor alternative in non-computer use. The latest government style manual recommends following Australian dictionaries in spelling choices.

The government should follow its own house style regardless of who is in power and what preferences individual politicians might have. This attempt on the part of the bureaucracy to curry favour with the PM by adopting –*mme* is ludicrous and time wasting.

The wrong 'pronounciation'

Intuitively we feel that the noun formed from the verb *pronounce* should be 'pronounciation' and until the early 18th century this would have been considered perfectly acceptable. But there were a lot of language purists in the 18th century who 'tidied up' English. They argued that *pronounce* came from Anglo-French and was correct, but *pronunciation* came from Latin *pronuntio* and should be *pronunciation*. We have all struggled with this but have more or less held the line on this distinction without entirely understanding the reason for it. Lately the number of people in the community who are quite convinced that 'pronounciation' is correct seems to have grown, and this is causing a younger generation to waver.

The Queen's English

The story is told that in 1586 Elizabeth I of England wrote to James VI of Scotland, and in that letter she penned the words *desiar* and *wold*. King James responded with *desyre* and *desire*, and *woulde* and *would*. Which just goes to show what a modern man he was. It is true that no one would have chivvied either writer about their spelling. No one would have dared but equally, no one would have bothered. The small group of people who were able to read and write did so with a highly idiosyncratic approach to spelling.

So what changed? The first thing that influenced the standardisation of spelling was the printing press. Basically, whatever spelling confronted the typesetter, he imposed his own, because it was easier.

This still doesn't explain today's attitudes to spelling.

The typesetter's reason for standardisation was practical, and inflicted no pain on the writer. There is no whiff of religious zeal emanating from printer William Caxton or his followers. Zeal entered with mass education which, on the one hand, offered ideals of literacy and, on the other, punishments for falling short of those ideals. The upside of standardisation is efficiency. The downside is obsession. There is no proof that ruthlessly standardised spellings result in greater ease of communication, although these days, because of our heightened awareness, any type of misspelling on the page is likely to distract us from the content. But if we weren't so sensitised, would we be so easily distracted?

The 19th century was the golden age of spelling rules – attempts to find patterns in English spelling which inevitably founder on the shoals of exceptions, and they founder because English is riddled with fragments of patterns of other languages from which it has borrowed words.

If we have come to assume that a good thought can only ever be couched in standard spelling, then surely we have taken the whole thing a little too far. If manners maketh the man, then good spelling maketh the writer. But remember, there is many a contemporary writer whose spelling had to be put in place by a sympathetic and discreet editor.

It's almost as if some of us would shrug our shoulders if we gained the reputation for being cruel to children and animals, just as long as it was generally known that we never made a spelling error.

I'm not advocating a return to the days of Queen Elizabeth. Standardised spelling prevents a lot of time wasting and wilfulness. There are many situations where it is admirable for writers to present a united front – in newspapers, in the various publications of a particular publishing company, in a book written by more than one author – and a generally agreed standard, particularly one that is easily accessible in dictionaries and style guides, saves a lot of argument. These days a confusion of spellings would be regarded as indefensible. To thrash out preferred spellings on an ad hoc basis would be a nightmare. But I wish the image of standard spelling was that of a trusty staff on which we lean rather than a rod to break our backs.

In today's educational climate there is a new emphasis on spelling as a tangible proof of education – proof of competence in writing, an ability to think, possibly even a passport to heaven. Since worth is so often a nebulous quality, it is convenient to have this one tangible indication that conveniently lends itself to efficient assessment. In a world where red pens glitter like knives in the censorial sun, children must be taught to spell for their own safety.

Rape goes colloquial

I had a most unusual request from an ABC radio presenter. It seems that the word *rape* has acquired various colloquial meanings, which sparked a discussion as to whether this weakened the abhorrence of the community towards the act of rape.

I argued that the colloquial use of *rape* followed the pattern of use of *massacre* and *murder*, both of which could mean 'defeat overwhelmingly' in a sports context. And that the language community was clever enough to cope with the seriousness of the basic meaning while at the same time employing the word in a different register and context with a different meaning. *Rape* was causing a shock because it was new. *Murder* and *massacre* had become unremarkable because the usage was common.

My fellow speaker disagreed completely. For her any meaning other than the basic one was a watering down of the act of violence. Someone texted to say that the act should not be confused with the word. Someone else texted to say that such words should not be in the dictionary, so we had the whole range of points of view.

The appeal of regionalism

Nostalgia is a powerful emotion and can attach itself to many things – a familiar object, a tune not heard for many a long day, a word from a place where we once belonged.

So the stranger in a foreign land of the *autotray* can be brought up short by encountering the old familiar *traymobile*. For those not familiar with either of these terms, *autotray* is what the Victorians call the *traymobile* of New South Wales – a small table on wheels, used for serving food, carrying plates, etc.

This is the attraction of regionalism – it reminds us strongly of what the world was like, what *we* were like when we were young. Even now I look out the window and identify the black-and-white bird in the garden as a *peewee*. My Victorian counterpart would think fondly of the *magpie lark*. I had *peanut butter* on toast but a Queenslander would have had *peanut paste*.

Regionalism attaches itself not just to words but to accent as well. There are those who claim that they can tell a Melburnian from a Queenslander, a West Australian from a Sydneysider. The most extreme example in Australia is the distinctive way South Australians pronounce the vowel in *school*.

Sometimes we seem to pursue regionalism with a fervour that goes beyond childhood nostalgia, almost with a desire to promote difference for its own sake. There is the hint of a claim that not only are we different but that we are better. That turns harmless regionalism into a kind of backyard jingoism.

In the short history of white settlement in this county we had only a brief opportunity to develop different kinds of English in different parts of the country before distances contracted and communications became nationwide. The tang of regionalism was, if not obliterated, then at least smoothed out by the national standard.

If asked to produce regionalisms we tend to dust off words that are part of the colonial period of our history and now form regional stereotypes that can be paraded as names of football teams or slogans on licence plates but which have no real life left in them.

Would I talk about *sandgropers* and *croweaters* except in self-conscious jest? I certainly do not describe myself as a *cornstalk*. Is one state's *devon* still another's *fritz*, and yet another's *polony*? Or has the might of the food retailers brought conformity to this humble sausage? Does anyone still wheel out either a *tray-mobile* or an *autotray*? It is probable that regionalism lurks unheard and unseen by our national organs of communication as too local and too domestic to be of interest.

Nevertheless it may still survive in the oral tradition or in the communications for small-scale local consumption – the meeting notes of clubs, societies and school associations, the messages on bulletin boards in supermarkets and halls. There has been too little research in this field for us to make any certain pronouncements.

The need to discuss matters of national import in the national standard has driven regionalism into discourse that is personal and intensely local. But I see no reason why there should not remain a desire for particularity and creativity within such a group that would give rise to new coinages. The next regionalisms that we identify and share may well come from this evolving reality.

How broad can the definition of a river be?

Until recently the definition of a river in the *Macquarie Dictionary* followed a traditional line. It read: 'a considerable natural stream of water flowing in a definite course or channel or series of diverging and converging channels'. Over various editions we have pondered these definitions and thought how little they related to the facts of Australian geography, how much we were influenced by our British inheritance. We looked out on the reality of Australian rivers and yet felt obliged to retain an essential British definition. By the time we arrived at the fourth edition the definition had changed somewhat. A river now is 'a defined watercourse of considerable size and length, whether flowing or dry according to the seasons, and whether a single channel or a number of diverging or converging channels'. The problem is, of course, to get a definition that captures both the Murray and the Todd, the former being always full of water (well, so far at least) and the latter rarely.

The definition of a river has legal consequences. When Australia was claimed for Britain, all the law that applied in England applied here too. But the English law was written from experience of English geography and climate. A river in England always has a bank and flowing water. Developers in Australia have been able to argue that rivers that are dry for at least part of the year do not count, according to the legal definition. It is another reminder of the curious ways in which words can shape our lives. Australia keeps having to shift the substance of the words we have inherited to match the Australian experience.

Shakespeare neologisms

From time to time a story surfaces about the number of words that Shakespeare created and added to the English language. One figure tossed around on the internet is 1700.

The first two in this list that I looked up in the OED were *premeditated* and *accused*. Both had earlier citations.

I believe that Shakespeare shifted words from one grammatical category to another and made up derived forms because both strategies helped with the smooth flow of the verse schema. A word like *horrid* interested me because that is a shift in meaning from the earlier meaning of 'shaggy or rough' but even here there is an earlier citation. It was perhaps a fashionable use of his day that he picked up and used in *Twelfth Night*. Author David Crystal should have consulted his OED before he added them to the Shakespeare list. The whole thing is complicated by the fact that a lexicographer like Johnson consulted only written texts and, of course, high in prestige among written texts were Shakespeare's plays so the first citation may well appear to come from Shakespeare even though the word was in common use at the time or even earlier.

Continuing to browse the list I came across *Anthropophagian*. This is an ad hoc derived form from *Anthopophagi*, a supposed race of cannibals. Shakespeare (or his character in *The Merry Wives of Windsor*) was making an allusion to a bit of folklore.

The form *lonely* does have the first citation as being from Shakespeare, although *lone* the adjective has a much longer history, and so deriving an adverbial form from *lone* is not such a big step. And we have to bear in mind that this is the first written citation. The word *lonely* may have been around generally at the time.

I do think that Shakespeare rolled language around to suit his purposes in a way that was admirable. He could give a word zing by changing its form or part of speech in ways that are always available to us in English though not many of us have the wit or the courage to take advantage of them. He picked up on some unusual items and maybe occasionally created a few. The Shakespeare neologisms camp overstates their case and gives the impression that the bard sat chewing the end of his quill (what a thought!) making up 1700 brand-new words. This is not the case.

Sorry to be such a sceptic!

Send it down Hughie

I made the mistake of being overly impressed by a historian's detailed analysis of the origin of this phrase. He, in turn, had been very interested in a family who explained that their ancestor, John Ziegler Huie, had been manager on a station near Narrandera in the late 19th century. Apparently he had the habit, at the approach of rain clouds, of firing off an old cannon full of shot in an attempt to seed the clouds. This would be accompanied by a chorus from the family of 'Send it down Huie'.

In retrospect there are a few things wrong with this as the origin of the phrase. If the prayer was to the station manager on the ground, the phrase should have been 'bring it down', not 'send it down'. And the level of formality in addressing the manager by his surname is unbelievable.

There is an even greater difficulty. The prayer is these days addressed to Hughie but there are earlier citations for 'Davey', 'Steve' and 'Jimmy'.

A correspondent to *The Bulletin* of 1912 records the phrase in the context of shearing and says that he heard it first in Narrandera where he believed it had originated. This supports the Narrandera link, but he goes on to say that it came from a Mr Huie, an amateur meteorologist who had great luck in predicting rain.

Other weather forecasters are given the credit. I have been told about a weather announcer in Perth who became well known for the intensity of the weather events he forecasted.

There was also an MP from Bendigo (called Hughie) who envisaged an irrigation scheme for Victoria, the phrase being interpreted as a reference to his labours. This appeared in *The World's News* (Sydney) 1946:

> *One explanation is that it is a corruption of the cry 'Lok ah shuie,' with which Chinese in the early days of the Victorian goldfields greeted the rain. 'Shuie' became gradually changed to 'Hughie.'*

WH Downing's *Digger Dialects* gives 'Send it down Steve' and notes that *Steve* was 'a common designation for a casual acquaintance', someone whose name you didn't know so you referred to him as Steve. In the context of the army the prayer was made so that marches, drills, etc., would be put off.

I found a citation in 1882 that sheds some light. In a report on a downpour of rain, a correspondent to the newspaper says: 'Old Jupiter Pluvius didn't stay to send it down gently, but appeared to throw it at us in a very promiscuous manner'. Jupiter Pluvius was the name given to Jupiter in ancient Rome, in his capacity as 'sender of rain'. This is a somewhat literary allusion.

It seems clear that in all cases the phrase is an appeal to a deity in command of the rain who is being asked to send it down from the heavens. I remember my father addressing the sky in a jocular fashion, again at the first sound of rain. Perhaps the joke lies in the great familiarity in the form of address – calling the god by his first name – Steve, Jimmy, Davey and finally Hughie.

In the case of John Ziegler Huie, the joke may have had extra spice because of the overlap of the names. Children, in the way of children, heard the expression uttered with evident enjoyment by their elders and assumed that the Hughie being addressed was the station manager. Their Huie since they knew no other.

Is there a shizzum in your shedyool?

I'm a 'skizzum' person myself so I have 'skedyools'. You can look at these different pronunciations in a number of ways. If we take *schism* first, the original form of the word from Greek was *scism* (with an *sk* pronunciation) but the spelling and pronunciation were aligned with Late Latin – an *sch* spelling and *sh* in the pronunciation. If you favour the Greek root you will take the hard *sk* pronunciation. If you know your Church Latin you will prefer the *sh* pronunciation. The situation is further confused by the fact that Webster threw his weight behind the Greek root and favoured the *sk* pronunciation while keeping the *sch* spelling. These days we often perceive the difference as a British/US variation rather than a Greek root/Late Latin variation. The word *schedule* did have an early existence in English as *scedule* but this spelling was revised to bring it in line with the Late Latin form. The pronunciation followed a similar pattern to *schism*.

Short-lived words

There are words that have a brief vogue and then fade away, largely because they are too dependent on an association with a particular person or event. For a short time *Stuart Diver* was rhyming slang for 'survivor' and *to do a Bradbury* meant 'to have an unexpected victory'. For a while people in Victoria were *Jeffed*, that is, sacked courtesy of Jeff Kennett or others in the same mould. But somehow these associations were too brief to last. Compare *a barry of a day* (a shocker of a day), which seems to carry on even when we have lost the association with entertainer Barry Crocker.

Sometimes the rules of the game change, leaving an expression high and dry. The first Gulf War gave us the verb *to scud* meaning 'to annihilate' literally or metaphorically. But the war was short and the expression quickly self-scudded. The *Slutzkin scheme* (named after Alan Slutzkin who was the subject of a court case to test the validity of the activity) was hung out to dry by the change in taxation laws. For a while we could think of nothing else but *dry Slutzkins* or *wet Slutzkins*, aka bottom-of-the-harbour schemes, but now there is not a Slutzkin left in the waters of taxation.

My political favourite is *incentivation*, which was a word that was stillborn. Foisted onto the Australian people by John Howard in the election campaign of 1987, it failed to capture the imagination of the community. And yet *incentivation* lives somewhere as the ghost of a word that we vaguely remember.

The other classic in this field is *multifunctionpolis*. For a short time in the late 1990s it was the city of the future. We were going to have one – perhaps in Adelaide, perhaps in the Hunter Valley, but we were not going to be left behind. It was always a strange notion – that the people who needed good wiring would all get together in brand-new glass skyscrapers to send lightning-fast communications to each other. We have moved past that to the belief that we all need good wiring and we need it now. And so the sun set on the mighty silicon heart of the multifunctionpolis even before a 20th-century Wordsworth could celebrate it with an Ode.

Simplified spelling

The Simplified Spelling Society formed in 1908. More than a hundred years later they are probably wondering how long it will take to bring about any kind of spelling reform in English. Other languages have done it – Chinese, Dutch. Other languages have beautifully regulated relations between sound and spelling – Japanese, Italian. But English went wrong with the combined effects of William the Conqueror who brought with him all things French including their spelling system, and the Great Vowel Shift that happened in English from the 14th to the 16th century. I would like to see a monument somewhere to the Great Vowel Shift, with people pausing in contemplation and respectfully removing their hats. It seems to warrant it. Actually it was a sound change that affected long stressed vowels. For example, the long *i* in *fine* in Middle English sounded like Italian *fino* but changed to *fine* rhyming with *align*. And once one vowel moved they all had to move to avoid confusion.

With all this, English has never recovered the sound-to-letter relationships that it had in the days of Old English. This certainly presents challenges to those learning English spelling and there is a lot of force in the argument that this should be corrected to the benefit of English personkind. The problem is really a political one. To get this to happen it would be necessary to get a super committee of all the varieties of English together, have them agree on whose accent would dictate spelling and send them back into their language communities with the power to enforce it. There will always be those in the community of a conservative nature who would resist change, and, for a short time at least, there would be an uncomfortable generational divide. We are unfortunately all so attached to our spellings, even if they are stupid!

The attraction of slang

The reason we like slang is that it represents the youthful period of language, sometimes slick and sometimes crude, but always aiming at that moment of focused linguistic inspiration.

I don't mean to imply that slang is solely the province of the young, although there is a juxtaposition of creative urges that means that we often associate slang with the up-and-coming generation. But the need to say things that are new, or to recycle old ideas in a new and vivid way can be confronted equally by young and old.

By comparison, standard and formal registers can be regarded as middle-aged respectability, the desire to shock replaced by the desire to conform, the linguistic equivalent of deciding that it is time to eat fibre for breakfast and take out private health insurance.

Slang is a response to a need to be innovative combined with the desire to live life dangerously, to flaunt the power of the word, to demonstrate a particular kind of style.

We worry about Australian English as a whole being swamped by American English, but when it comes to our slang that anxiety becomes acute. The old-style slang of Barry Humphries and Paul Hogan seems somewhat dated in the new millennium but what do we have to replace it? The language of Bart and Homer Simpson, of *South Park*, of *Seinfeld*, of *Sex and the City*? We can add to this such items as 'Bazinga!' from *The Big Bang Theory*, 'Winter is coming!' from *Game of Thrones*, and the stunning contribution of 'Amazeballs!' made by Perez Hilton.

It is easy to see how our current slang is so derivative. Much of it happens first in American English and filters through to us. What happens, happens there first. There's really not much left for us to do.

Except that there is still the experience of being an Australian, of being in this place, in this society, in this culture, for which we have to find the right words. It is an Australia heavily influenced by America, but not wholly overrun. We have to have ownership of the words we use. Even the hand-me-downs have to become integrated into a discourse that is distinctively Australian.

We follow, we copy, but every now and then we have to do our own thing because there is no one else who can name the names and set the style. Look at Aussie Rules, look at the Aussie tradition of horseracing, look at the beach. Look at the following words recorded by children in Alice Springs, in which local colour is evident:

biggest mobs a lot
Comical Railways Commonwealth Railways
galah session a radio talkback session
ju-ju lips lips that are protruding
muchanic a person who is a bush mechanic who knows a lot about nothing and a little bit about something of engines
snotty gobbles red, white and black fruit of some acacia bushes
twin-stickin' her when the truckies let go of the steering wheel and grab for both gear sticks
Charlie Queenie-Queenie a small bug, lives in soft sands (ant-lion)
donkey beetles hard-shelled beetles common in Alice Springs district

A nice definition of slang has appeared in Jonathon Green's dictionary, *Cassell's Dictionary of Slang*. He gives the origin of the word as 'the Scandinavian "sleng", which also renders standard English's "sling", and means "a slinging", "a device", "a strategy"'. Thus slang is both literally and figuratively a 'slung' or 'thrown' language, tossed cunningly, as it were, into the hearer's face and ears.

Green also maintains that slang is above all 'the language of the city – urgent, pointed, witty, cruel, capable of both excluding and including, of mocking and confirming'. This may be true of this day and age, but slang is an aspect of a fully functioning variety of English wherever it occurs, flourishing perhaps where the centre of gravity of a community might be and therefore as often as not flourishing in the city. In colonial times, where the city/bush equation was more equally balanced, slang was as much a part of bush life as of city life. It is also true to say that city slang is more often recorded, and the slang of marginal communities more often than not ignored.

This leads us to some of the defining features of Australian slang, which in popular belief is recognised for two attributes, the first being its black humour and pervasive irony, its constant downplaying of events and downsizing of people. The second is its reportedly huge range and vast lexicon.

The black humour comes from its colonial origins, where grim humour was a strategy for coping with grim situations. It is particularly evident in phrases allowing for an allusive surprise such as the following found at the headword *useful* in the *Macquarie Book of Slang*:

useful as a bucket under a bull
useful as a dead dingo's donger
useful as a dry thunderstorm
useful as a glass door on a dunny
useful as an arsehole on a broom
useful as an ashtray on a motorbike
useful as a piss in a shower
useful as a pocket on a singlet
useful as a roo bar on a skateboard
useful as a sore arse to a boundary rider
useful as a spare dick at a wedding
useful as a submarine with screen doors
useful as a third armpit
useful as a wart on the hip
useful as a wether at a ram sale
useful as a witch's tit
useful as the bottom half of a mermaid
useful as tits on a bull
useful as two knobs of billy goat poop

216

The belief that Australians have more slang at their disposal than any other English language community possibly springs from the Australian habit of using slang in situations where other cultures would stick to a formal register. This has the effect of making Australian slang more notable and noted. A moment's reflection on the wealth of American slang would make one query the pre-eminence of Aussie slang. There is no scientific measurement of language varieties in these terms but it would seem that we are all equally gifted in all the registers of our variety.

Australian English is still building on its heritage. For example, *tucker fucker* is a term used initially for a cook, particularly the kind of second-rate cook who churned out meals where cheap food in bulk was required and no one asked too many questions about the standard of cooking, such as in institutions and economy-run boarding schools. In modern times, the meaning has been extended in two directions. It has become both a colloquial name for tomato sauce, sometimes expanded to *tucker fucker upper*, and for the microwave. Both for obvious reasons.

We borrow, we adapt, we interpret, we bend things to our use. It's a skill that we should be proud of.

It's probably Australian culture. The end result is still a unique Australian blend and a unique Australian view.

SMSing

SMS stands for 'Short Messaging Service' and it refers to the system whereby mobile phone users can communicate via text messages, using the keypad of the phone to key the messages in and the screen to read them.

Different categories of shorthand have emerged to facilitate the speedy keying of messages within the space restrictions that often apply.

A basic technique is to take extremely common expressions of a functional nature, which can be severely coded because the resulting initialisms will be easily remembered. The basic form of coding is that the first letter of each word is given, often capitalised.

BRB	Be right back
HAND	Have a nice day
BTW	By the way
ATB	All the best

A syllable that has the sound of a number can be so coded, and a syllable that has the sound of a letter of the alphabet can be so coded.

CUL8R	*See you later*
F2F	*Face-to-face*
GR8	*Great*

Phrases that are not of the highest frequency may need more than an initial letter to be understood. In such cases the shape of the word is given, the first letter being capitalised and the other letter or letters lower case. Words can be run together with the capital marking the start of a new word, as in:

JstCllMe	*Just call me*
MsULkeCrZ	*Miss you like crazy*
DoUCmHrOftn?	*Do you come here often?*

Long vowels may be differentiated from short vowels by capitalisation.

In the instance GtItRIt, the 'Gt' marks the beginning and ending of 'Get', the 'I' marks the beginning of 'It', the 'R' marks the beginning of 'Right' and the capital 'I' indicates the long 'i' in *right* as opposed to lower case 'i', which would be pronounced as in *bit*.

GtItRIt	*Get it right*
DoUAgrE	*Do you agree?*

Capitalisation may also be used to mark a double vowel or consonant, as in:

DoUACpt?	*Do you accept?*
Dar2BDFrnt	*Dare to be different*

Other well-known abbreviations or symbols can be incorporated, or some visual feature captured, in a kind of SMS word play, as in:

XMeQk	*Kiss me quick* (the 'X' represents a kiss)
ShtYaiis	*Shut your eyes* (the double letter 'i' represents two eyes)
KX	*A thousand kisses* (the letter 'X' represents a kiss and the letter 'K' represents '1000')

SMS also allows for indications of moods, attitudes and reactions.

ROFL	*Rolling on the floor laughing*
[EG]	*Evil grin*
H&K	*Hugs and kisses*
E2EG	*Ear-to-ear grin*
^5	*High five*
T+	*Think positive*

Emoticons perform this function also. Some common emoticons are:

:-)	*Smiley*
:-O	*Surprised*

This non-verbal use of characters may also be extended to the fanciful representation of objects, people, situations, etc.

@-->->--	*Rose*
{:-)	*Person wearing a toupee*
:-B)	*Having a cold*
<|:o)>	*Clown*

Will SMS take over our English? I don't think so. We do incorporate popular items as slang words in English. Will the code 'tmoz' for 'tomorrow', become the colloquial word *tmoz* with an intuitive pronunciation, so that we can use it in speech as well as in writing? Those of us who spend a lot of time texting will find it harder to see the boundary between texting and standard writing. The same is true of the difficulty that some people have seeing the boundary between colloquial register and formal register. Some people handle the concept of appropriate language well, others stumble along with one style to fit all. I don't think any of this amounts to the death of the English language as we know it.

The soirée is in again

Have you noticed? It is fashionable to attend soirées. The rules are that you are lightly entertained as you are lightly supplied with food and drink at an hour approximating high tea. In the London of Charles Dickens the soirée was so popular that it ended up going from upmarket to downmarket, much to the amusement of the cognoscenti who mimicked the pronunciation of the populace and referred to such occasions as 'swarries'. The term pops up in Henry Lawson where, as in London, the emphasis was on the lavishness of the spread rather than the quality of the entertainment. A 'cold swarry' (that is, where cold meats were served) was given the thumbs down. So enjoy the swarry. Before you know it, we will be having conversaziones and colloquiums again but be prepared to undergo those without benefit of food or drink.

The sounds of Australian English

One of the heroes of Australian lexicography is Professor Alex Mitchell who, in 1942, deliberately provoked an argument in the press about the Australian accent. He was asked to advise the ABC, the national broadcaster, on what was an acceptable accent for ABC presenters to have. Mitchell set the cat among the pigeons by saying, very publicly in an article headed *There Is Nothing Wrong with Australian Speech*, in the *ABC Weekly* 1942, that:

> *We should use an Australian speech, without apology and without any sense of a need for self-justification. There is nothing wrong with the Australian voice or speech. It is as acceptable, as pleasant, as good English, as any speech to be heard anywhere in the English-speaking commonwealth.*

This was a strong counter to the chorus of voices complaining about the Australian accent. Popular belief held that we spoke the way we did because there were so many flies in the bush that we had learned to speak with our mouths shut – the lazy lips syndrome. Another view was that, as we suffered so constantly from bronchitis from dust and grass seeds blowing in the wind, we had developed a permanent nasalisation. This most unpleasant feature of our speech was seen as a marker of the broad Australian accent that carried a lot of social baggage with it. The broad accent is now the minority accent in Australia, with a general accent and an educated accent being the two major forms. All participants in the Mitchell debate were united in their hatred of the modified Australian accent, the one that tried to be oh-so-English and ended up being neither English nor Australian. That, too, is now a thing of the past. Mitchell succeeded in making the Australian accent acceptable to the national broadcaster, and for this we are grateful to him.

Speaking the same language

The Tower of Babel is a powerful story – human arrogance brought low by divine retribution. If we had not attempted to reach God we might all be speaking the same language.

There have been attempts to regain the pre-Babel state with contrived universal languages such as Esperanto. It is argued that humankind almost achieved it with Latin in the Middle Ages but that was a rather limited kind of universality where the rich and powerful shared a common language in the small bit of the world that mattered, from a European point of view.

Linguistics tells a different story to explain the diversity of languages. If you suppose that you have a group of people speaking the same language, and by some magic you impose a mountain range right down the middle of the group, then you will end up first of all with two different dialects, then, over time, with two different languages.

The reason for this is that each group responds to different pressures for change – partly external pressures, partly internal.

The external pressure is the physical and social environment. Suppose that one side of the mountain range is desert and the other side is rainforest. And that one group is a democracy and the other is a dictatorship. Undoubtedly, the lexicon required by each group to express their circumstances is going to be markedly different.

But there is another force at work that is not nearly as obvious or dramatic. On each side, the communities make day-to-day decisions on language issues that arise naturally from the language system in which they operate. Let's say that the hot topic on each side of the mountain happens to be the spelling of *miniscule/minuscule* and the use of *protest* as a transitive verb as in 'to protest a decision'. One side decides in favour of *miniscule* and the transitive *protest*, the other decides against.

The cumulative effect of all these different decisions made in isolation of each other results in the two groups speaking different languages.

The process can be accelerated by fashion. There are choices that arise naturally, and there are choices that we engineer for no reason other than to perfect our self-image. It works in language as it does in clothes. We choose to be the sort of person who says 'Cool!' or the sort of person who says 'Amazeballs!'.

Constructed languages that attempt to restore mutual intelligibility to the world have worked only in very precise circumstances. Airline pilots speak a functional universal English but its range is limited to a very specific context. There is a universal sign language for tourists but it, too, has a limited repertoire – entrance and exit, luggage, food and drink, and the location of toilets. Even this demonstrates style choices which surprise us – the walking man with the 1930s hat seems to be limited to parts of Europe while the same man without the hat appears in others.

There is a suggestion that English might achieve, by sheer weight of numbers and spread of use, the critical mass needed to take over the world. This is entirely speculative since we are still a long way from such a state of affairs and there are other contenders for this role.

Would it be desirable for English (or another language for that matter) to achieve this kind of dominance? Some would argue that this is analogous to a beautiful flower becoming a weed with devastating effects on the language ecology in other habitats.

If indeed the world did speak one language, would the linguistic cost matter? It depends on whether you think that what follows on from a universal language is greater understanding, harmony and peace. The sceptic in me says that is not necessarily so.

Finding an
international spelling

In spelling, a little knowledge is a dangerous thing. We learn how to spell *precede* and *intercede* and so we go on to align *supersede* with them because it sounds like a *-cede* word, arriving at the spelling *supercede* and not realising that the etymology of *supersede* is quite different. The *-cede* words relate to the Latin *cedere* 'to go' so *precede* is literally 'to go before', *intercede* 'to go between', whereas *supersede* relates to the Latin *supersedere*, literally 'to sit above'.

Making false patterns in spelling is a trap that we can all fall into, as is not remembering the peculiarities of words that have been borrowed into English from some other language. This is standard fare. To combat these problems there is a range of opinions, ranging from those who advocate wholesale spelling reform, to those who think that we should just give in on the words that are most commonly misspelled, like *consensus* and *inoculate*, and live with them in their new shape (*concensus* and *innoculate*).

There is a third camp developing in this spelling debate and that is the group who would like the world not to be split between American and British spelling. This group would like us to arrive at some kind of international standard. A dictionary enthusiast suggested that I should set up an international committee to determine the English spelling of the future.

This did play into my occasional fantasy about being nominated as the Great Australian Native English Speaker who could resolve all disputes within Australian English on spelling and usage with my personal fiat. Why not extend it to being the Native Speaker of the Globe – the Galaxy, the Cosmos even?

While it is true that English spelling is a curse, and while I would like the overseas trips, there are two obvious difficulties. One is that language communities are wedded to their chosen spellings, the ones they are taught, the ones they grew up with and espouse as intrinsic to their notions of their kind of English. The other is that the chances of either of the two big Englishes listening to Australian English on how they should lift their game are so remote that my fantasy crumpled.

Valerie Yule, a Melbourne literacy expert, offered a stick for walloping the big Englishes – that they are being totally unfair. English is now in the mouths of a lot of people in the world who are not native speakers of British or American English, and not even native speakers of English at all. It is not right to inflict on these people the oddities and eccentricities of varieties, which, in demographic terms, are now outnumbered by speakers of English around the globe. These oddities present serious difficulties for people learning English for a better life. What bullies the prestige Englishes are!

In the past I have ignored all cries for spelling reform but it seems to me that this need for an international standard is one that we will feel increasingly. It is possible that the mood will grow for some kind of rational approach. What I would like to avoid is the endless theorisation and bickering that I can see would engulf such an attempt if we were to develop a standard from scratch. What I think we should do is immediately adopt Canadian spelling. Here we have a community that has suffered even more than we have from the squeeze of an English past and an American present. They have therefore produced the best synthesis of the two spelling codes and have arrived at the most sensible solutions.

Go Canadian – that's my advice.

Standards in English

What do you do when you are confronted by such slippages in the English language as 'in agreeance with' for 'in agreement with' and 'aks' instead of 'ask'?

The idea that language changes are a matter of popular will, that acceptance can be forced on a minority who are correct by the sheer weight of numbers of the incorrect majority, is one that is still displeasing to some people, who see it as the path to a decay of standards.

If enough people say 'I'm in agreeance with you' without even suspecting that there might be something wrong with this usage, then is it right that there should be no argument in the language court of law?

I see no sign that *agreeance* is a passing aberration, which might in a timely way be addressed and corrected. You care? Of course you do. The whole idea is abhorrent. But before you let rip with some thunderous condemnations, bear in mind that lexicographer Henry Fowler at the beginning of the 20th century listed *enthuse, orate* and *liaise* as backformations that had not yet achieved respectability. By the end of that century no one would have suspected that those words had anything other than a legitimate origin.

So what are your rights in the matter?

Firstly, to maintain your own practice – until such time as you yourself feel happy about changing it.

Secondly, to identify as erroneous those changes that are still not accepted by the community at large.

Rights go with obligations, and in this case the obligation is to accept as a legitimate variation those changes that *are* accepted by the community at large. The guide to what is and what isn't 'accepted' will be the accumulated wisdom of the dictionaries, style guides and language reference written by speakers of your kind of English for the use of your language community.

The dictionary cannot dictate to you what your choice is in the matter but it can give you guidance on how relenting or unrelenting your opposition should be to a particular usage. This is of particular significance if you happen to be in a position to have influence on others in these matters, if you are perhaps a teacher or an editor, or even just a parent attempting to maintain good relations with your children.

It is amusing that while the change in English from Old English through Chaucerian English to Modern English doesn't seem to trouble us, change in our own lifetime can be extremely unsettling. We think that 'Whan that Aprille with his showres soote, the droght of March hath perced to the rote' is charming and so musical. But we come down like a ton of bricks on changes happening today.

The conservatives amongst us have a role to play in deciding these issues – no language community should rush into expressions like 'in agreeance with' without a bit of a struggle. But neither should they feel that they have a monopoly on language standards, and that the rules that they learnt and the choices that they made when they were young should be regarded as unalterable truth by the next generation.

Strange phrases

Reinterpretations of phrases are sometimes cringe-making. The expression *give someone free rein* has overnight become *give someone free reign*, and it seems as if no one has noticed. Are we so unfamiliar with horses that we cannot even imagine what it is like to drop the reins and let the horse have its head? Rather we have to invent this strange monarch with liberal powers who gives free reign. There are many, many citations in otherwise impeccable text. And none of those people who ring the ABC or write to the *Macquarie Dictionary* have even begun to build up a head of steam about it. It has just happened without comment.

We are also liable to error in our analysis of words and phrases that we have heard but never seen written down. We *hone in* rather than *home in* because we were not quite sure whether we heard an *m* or an *n*. And if we needed a satisfactory 'origin' of the phrase, we can call up the whittler peeling away the layers to arrive at the core. There are a number of floating errors in the community that have arisen in this way: *an elegant sufficiency* becomes *an eloquent sufficiency* because *eloquent* has overlaid *elegant*; we order an *expresso* instead of an *espresso*; we fall into the trap of *could of* and *should of* because we have misheard *could've* and *should've*.

Fulsome praise is re-analysed as 'praise that is full', and ceases to mean 'overblown and insincere praise' but rather 'complete and whole-hearted praise'. The *hoi polloi* are no longer 'the masses' but rather 'the high and mighty'.

In phrases where there is one unfamiliar word, we have a dreadful tendency to replace it with a word we know. So *one fell swoop* becomes *one foul swoop*. *Fell* is a rare word these days so we search for a more familiar replacement. *Foul* sounds like *fell* – just the difference of a vowel, and the meaning fits, although a better synonym would be *menacing*. These are blatant and common errors, but the slips we make can be quite unexpected and quite eccentric. I knew someone who always said *stragetic* rather than *strategic*, as if a childhood error had been etched so deeply into his brain that he no longer heard the difference between the two. It's slightly unnerving to consider that the most experienced of writers can still be tripped up by these childhood misunderstandings.

The tall poppy syndrome

Now here's a little etymological folk tale that, as such tales often are, is both intriguing and improbable. The historian Livy tells us that Tarquin the Proud was bent on capturing the city of Gabii. As a softening-up exercise his son Sesto spent some time there, ingratiating himself with the citizens. Tarquin wanted to send Sesto a message that the time had come for him to start ridding the world of the leaders of Gabii, but how to send such an awkward message? No one could be trusted. As the chosen messenger watched, Tarquin started pruning the garden of the tallest poppies. The messenger, somewhat puzzled, reported the actions of Tarquin to Sesto, who put two and two together and went to work pruning the citizens of Gabii. The rest of the world regards the expression as an Australianism.

Tasmanian English

The heroic story from the Beaconsfield mine collapse in 2006 brought us all into contact, not only with mining terms that we might never have encountered before, but also with items that are peculiar to the brand of English that is spoken in Tasmania. The *crib room* was one mining term that had to be explained. The lexicon of Cornish miners dominates the mining industry in Australia. The original miners came to South Australia in the 1850s to mine the copper that was discovered there but they, with more reason and experience than anyone else, were drawn to the gold-fields of Bendigo and Ballarat and also to Tasmania.

These days we think of a crib as something that a baby sleeps in, but that sense goes back to the basic one of a latticed box full of hay for the animals. From there *crib* goes in two directions. One follows the line of bedding, housing, etc., while the other is all to do with food and is largely dialectal in English – Devonshire and Cornwall in particular. So the *crib* was a portion or fragment of food, carried in a *crib box* and eaten during the day. Miners ate their crib in a room deep in the mine that today has such luxuries as the showers that were the first port of call for the rescued miners.

Another Tasmanian habit that caught general attention was the use of *cock* as a form of greeting. 'G'day cock!' Tasmanians are wont to say. It seems strangely antiquated to mainlanders. Reminiscent of *old cock*, which sounds British and dates back to the 1600s. Similarly *rummin* meaning 'an odd character' (which probably even Tasmanians no longer analyse as 'a rum one') and *nointer* for a spoiled brat (from British dialect *anointer* 'a daredevil', that is, someone who needs 'anointing' or 'thrashing') – these are just a few instances of a scattering of terms that are preserved in the island state, some from convict times, some from colonial days, some from mining communities.

The War on Terror

The War on Terror had its impact on the English language. At a fairly mundane level we juggled *9/11* and *September 11*, settling on the latter as being more consistent with our system of writing dates. We tried to decide fairly and honestly whether we think that the use of *crusade* in this day and age and in this context is insensitive or not. And somehow in all of this the difference between a refugee and a terrorist became blurred, particularly when refugees were labelled *illegal immigrants*, *queue jumpers* and *boat people*. The term *asylum seeker* emerged as a neutral way out.

As we listened to radio reports it became clear that we were still not sure about the correct names of some of the main players. The following were some of the major points of difficulty.

There was some anxiety over the reference to Saddam Hussein as simply Saddam – was this perhaps an offensive familiarity? It seems that the Arab world does not think so, that Saddam was his given name whereas Hussein was the given name of his father. Moreover most Iraqis would refer to him as Saddam. What is of interest is the allegation that the first President Bush deliberately mispronounced his name, stressing the first syllable rather than the second. Pronounced Sa-DAM the meaning is 'one who confronts'; pronounced SA-dam the meaning is 'a barefoot beggar'. Fascinating as it is, I wonder if the first President Bush's Arabic was up to it.

There have been various attempts to pronounce Al Qaeda, a common one giving *Qaeda* two syllables and rhyming it with 'raider'. The ABC recommends a pronunciation in which *Qae-* is the stressed syllable and rhymes with 'high'. The word can be given two syllables or three as you prefer – so 'KIGHder' or 'KIGH-uh-der'.

Of course solving the language difficulties doesn't help with the politics, which are as murky as ever.

Tracking local words

Regional Australian English offers insights for the word detective or the word archaeologist. 'Detective' in that an analysis of this material involves hunting down obscure origins of words or phrases. 'Archaeologist' in that I need to dig down below the surface of contemporary Australian English to our language past.

Words like *teasy* and *cranky* are like the toes of a dinosaur left visible in today's language terrain. *Teasy*, used mostly with reference to babies and meaning 'fretful', is from Cornish dialect and was noted by a contributor from South Australia where Cornish dialect has left its mark. Cornish miners were recruited in the 1840s to mine the newly discovered copper deposits and introduced a certain number of dialectal terms into the English of that region. I have also found *teasy* in Wollongong, which is, of course, another mining town.

Cranky meaning 'eccentric' is another remnant of British English notably from Scottish and northern English dialect. It surfaces in south-eastern Victoria where a strong Scottish influence is discernible.

So much for the archaeology – now for the sleuthing. A number of people have mentioned *continental* as the name for a fundraising activity, usually starting early in the day with a fete or fair and continuing into the evening with a concert or dance. This was a common term in Adelaide but others remembered it from their childhood in country New South Wales. One Adelaidian dredged up a memory of the phrase *Continental Sunday* as being the kind of Sunday that the Irish and German community in Adelaide favoured and that the Anglo community regarded as a violation of the Sabbath.

It is amazing what information people have tucked away in odd corners of their brain. In the 1850s in England, the term *Continental Sunday* was used to describe a day of public entertainment that was common in France or on the Continent. It was contrary to how the English expected to spend their Sundays.

Transferred to colonial Australia this came to be restricted to the kind of public entertainment that was set up to raise funds for schools or charities. In that more narrow sense *continental* was used around Australia although we have yet to trace how far the use of the word spread.

Phrases are a rich source of creative variety in regional Australia. So often these are the optional extras of language where the base meaning is understood and the phrase indicates an intensity of feeling or is an opportunity to say something ear-catching.

For example, from Victoria we have *clumsy as a duck in a ploughed paddock*, which is surprisingly rural for urban Melbourne but quite a vivid image. Adelaide has contributed *hot enough for cotton frocks and plastic handbags*, a summery picture that is both old-fashioned and appealing. From Tasmania we have *a head like a busted sofa* to describe someone whose hair is wild and unkempt. And lastly from Melbourne we have a phrase used when saying goodbye. It is *Thank your mother for the rabbits*. Imagine explaining that to an outsider.

Exclamations are another fertile area since these noises of surprise, indignation, etc., carry more meaning in how they are said than in the actual words used. *Yickadee!* they say in the Northern Territory when they are extremely pleased. *Holy boon-boon!* they respond in some astonishment in Far North Queensland. *Gammon!* they say in North Queensland when they think you are pulling their leg. *Bunnies to that!* they say in Gippsland when they are feeling put-upon.

Greetings – hello and goodbye – are similarly a prime location for decorative touches. When in Adelaide, don't say 'hello', say *bonji!* In Northern Victoria *salada!* means 'farewell'. Many people have commented on the rural Australian *hoo-ray*, meaning 'goodbye', with both syllables given equal measure and the stress on the first syllable. It is therefore clearly differentiated from *hooray!* the expression of joy.

Fashion is also productive. Would you like to have a ginder? Before you answer that question you should perhaps know that a *ginder* is the word for a haircut in Bunbury, West Australia.

You may be familiar with the *Darwin rig* or *Territory rig*. In a part of the world where shorts and open-neck shirts are the standard dress, this ensemble dignifies official occasions – long trousers, shirt and tie. This use of rig ultimately relates to the configuration of masts, sails, etc., on a sailing ship, but by the 1840s was a colloquial reference to a set of clothes, an outfit.

There are various words for swimsuits – *bathers* from NSW through Victoria and South Australia to Western Australia, *cossie* in NSW and *togs* or *swimming togs* in Queensland. *Speedos* for men seem to have come in for special attention – *sluggos* in NSW, *ballhuggers* in

Perth and *dick togs* or *DTs* in Queensland. We all know about *budgie smugglers*.

Some of my favourite regionalisms are *wongi* – a borrowing from a West Australian Aboriginal language meaning 'a chat', *pimply squash* – 'a thick-skinned gourd covered with bumps', apparently not known south of Newcastle and *snot-block* – 'a vanilla slice'. I couldn't quite believe this last one, but I have been assured by a number of Victorians (mostly men) that it is perfectly correct. Indeed they are surprised that the rest of Australia doesn't use the term. I suspect that food terms are likely to bring the yuck factor with them but perhaps we retain a bit of yuck in our language to remind us of our childhood.

Trademarks

Every now and then in the haul of words that we casually pull in for the dictionary there is one of those strange fish labelled 'trademark'. Some of them are clearly identified as such – bright markings splashed across them and neon lights flashing – but on others the markings have faded and only those who are really attuned to these creatures remember that they began life as brand names.

Often what happens then is that a tug-of-war begins with the dictionary representing the language community on one side, and the company that originated the trademark on the other.

The *Macquarie Dictionary*'s policy on words that came into being as trademarks is to include them only if they function as generics. So the word *esky* appears in the dictionary because people use it without any sense of its being a trademark and apply it to any brand of portable icebox. *Esky* has given rise to the colloquial (and derogatory) expression *esky lidders* for boogie board riders, another sign that *esky* has a life of its own.

The problem is that there is no precise cut-off in the awareness of trademark status. It is a cline. So, a decade ago, a *coca-cola* could have meant either the particular drink with the Coca-Cola brand or what we would refer to now as any *cola drink*. This situation came about undoubtedly because Coca-Cola was so successful. It is what every trademark owner fears – too much success with the result that they lose control of the word they create. Coca-Cola reclaimed their brand and coached the marketplace to use *cola drink* (often shortened to *cola*) when they wanted a generic.

We have had some correspondence over *vaseline*, and duly undertook research on it in the supermarkets of this city where it is clear that the trademark term is *Vaseline* and the generic term is *petroleum jelly*. The other half of the research involved eliciting either *vaseline* or *petroleum jelly* from members of the general public who were asked what they called it, regardless of what brand they actually bought. Unfortunately, *vaseline* won hands down. I think that quite apart from the fact that Australians are unfamiliar with the name, *petroleum jelly* presents difficulties to a community that thinks of *jelly* as sweet, wobbly stuff that kids eat. *Gel* would have been more appropriate.

In the fourth edition we really stuck our necks out and included the term *google* as in *You can google for information on your homework topic*, or, *If you can't find any information, have a little google*. But can you google without using Google? The dictionary thinks you can. As ever, it is a tribute to the power of Google that this is the case. But it is both good and bad news for the holders of the Google trademark.

In assessing the situation with trademarks, each one has to be dealt with on its merits. The owners of the trademarks would like dictionary editors to remove their creations from the dictionary, but the words are in the dictionary precisely because they have escaped the control of the companies. Caterpillar contacted the *Macquarie* editors insisting that *caterpillar tracks* be removed. Amusingly, they included a transcript of a judge who talked about Caterpillar as the Rolls-Royce of treads! Rolls-Royce itself is upset about the expressions *a Rolls-Royce production* and *the Rolls-Royce of* such-and-such. So it goes.

If there is evidence that a word or phrase is used generically, then that use needs to be covered in the dictionary. The link to the trademark is then explained in the etymology because we are now dealing, not with the trademark itself, but with the word that derived from the trademark. Its origin needs to be explained just as much as does a word from Greek or Latin or Swahili.

The issue is the ownership of words. Here you have a little group, a company, that wants to control an aspect of language. Their dilemma is that the more successful they are – the more people use their word – the less control they are likely to have. Their strategies to keep control make fascinating reading. Recently we had the case of the *burqini*, an inspired coinage from an Australian swimwear producer that almost immediately was taken up by the community as a generic term. The creator of the burqini didn't know whether to be flattered that her word was so popular, or dismayed that she had lost control over it.

Obviously publication in the headword list of a dictionary is an indication that the word has reached generic status which is why it occasions such fuss. Sometimes the trademark owners abandon the struggle and invent a new one – take *biro* and Bic. Sometimes they fight, as did Coca-Cola. In all of this the dictionary is an interested bystander. Despite what the trademark owners think, there is nothing we can do that directly changes the situation. The battle has to be won by the trademark owners, and the means is to establish a different name for common use within the language community.

Typos

The bane of every writer's life! The problem is that we see what we are expecting to see, not what is actually there, particularly if we are caught up in the writing process and most of our brain is preoccupied with the meaning of what we are writing. It takes a particular style of reading to pick up typos, a reading in which you confine yourself to the surface of the page and not engage in the meaning of the text. Oddly enough, the bigger the type, the harder it is often to spot errors, as the Victoria Police Commissioner discovered when he unveiled a plaque at a new police station at Mooroopna, a small town near Shepparton. Unfortunately the plaque had *Moorpoopna*. Typos can be very amusing ('scared cows' for 'sacred cows') or appear to have a significance ('The Awful Government of Russia' as opposed to 'The Lawful Government of Russia'). They are fun in someone else's text. I just don't want them in my own.

A losing ugg

The sad story is that the gallant ugg boot, that unique Australian contribution to the footwear of the world, has lost a legal battle in the US. A judge has decided that the history of the word in Australia is irrelevant to its trademark status in the US which, to quote the lawyer for the Aussie ugg, 'effectively dismembered our case'. His opinion was that the judge was wrong but there is no arguing with a judge, at least not without a lot of money to throw around, so the parties settled. The case in Australia proceeded rather differently.

The word *ugg* seems to have appeared in Adelaide where the surfies felt the cold a little more keenly in winter. A local supplier of sheepskins had scraps left over that the surfies turned into improvised boots. From this the ugg boot was developed. But a Sydney surf shop owner picked up the idea and started selling the boots in Sydney. Not content with that he trademarked the name *ugg boot*. He should not have been allowed to do this because the name was already in general use in Adelaide and around Port Phillip, but presumably the office in Sydney had few contacts with southern surfies and granted the Sydney supplier the trademark. Later this trademark was sold to an American firm.

There are a number of theories about the origin of the name, but the best guess is that it is short for *ugly boot*.

It seems that the law in Australia has decided that *ugg boot* is a generic term and we can all use it freely, while the law in the US has decided that *ugg boot* as a name is the property of the company that bought it in good faith. Quite where this leaves Australian companies selling to American markets I am not sure, but at least in this country we can flaunt our ugg boots without fear.

Un-Australian

How do we get to be un-Australian? There are several answers. Entrepreneur John Singleton's remains the most succinct: 'It is un-Australian to drive past a pub'. Former politician Fred Daly's is, I'm afraid, rather dated: 'I suppose there is nothing more un-Australian than a tea-bag'. I have sympathy for this point of view. While I don't go so far as to swing the billy around my head at every morning tea-time to settle the tea leaves, I do prefer the old-fashioned pot with leaves in it to the tea bag. But I am conscious of being surrounded by battalions of tea bags claiming the support of middle Australia so I would be hard put to call them un-Australian. I also realise that the term *leaf tea* has come into existence precisely because tea bags are now the norm.

The Howard dictum was that we were un-Australian if we didn't have 'Australian values' (and I dread that term almost as much as *un-Australian* itself). Peter Costello lined up Australian values with the rule of law, democracy and a secular state, and that got us off to a flying start. Then John Howard derailed the word by linking it to what was taught in schools. Private schools apparently had Australian values in spades, Islamic schools had none and public schools were 'value-neutral', or, in other words, valueless. It all makes the debate on Asian values versus Western values relatively straightforward.

It did lead to a rethink of the dictionary entry for *un-Australian*. In its early 19th century use, this term carried with it the notion that the person tagged had primary loyalties that did not attach to the Australian nation but to some other country or institution. Thus communism was suspect because it was too international. Catholicism made one a servant of the Pope in Rome. Any ethnic background led to the suspicion that one's heart belonged to the country of one's birth. Australians were loyal to Australia. To be un-Australian was to be potentially capable of disloyalty.

In its later appearance in the 1990s, *un-Australian* degenerated to a smear word that could mean almost anything. The *Macquarie Dictionary* has difficulty with words that have zero denotation while being full bottle on connotation but the definition that tries to capture this reads: 'violating a pattern of conduct, behaviour, etc., which, it is implied by the user of the term, is one embraced by all Australians'. So if you think that the people who eat spinach are beyond the pale, then you can label spinach-eaters un-Australian. This carries with it the assumption that all Australians think the way you do and line up beside you in their loathing of the detestable spinach-eaters.

What makes you un-Australian changes with the times and with the speaker. It is almost too difficult for the dictionary to pin it down.

Underworld slang

A Nice Cup of Tea and a Gorilla was the heading for a newspaper report on the Wood Royal Commission. The article went on to explain that a *cup of tea* was a clandestine way of drinking alcohol by having it served in a teapot, and that a *gorilla* was a bribe of $1000. There was general surprise that the police and the criminals shared a patois, the intuitive belief being that a group that spoke in the same way probably thought in much the same way as well. Whose side were the cops on? The community's, or the people with whom they could talk the talk?

How far you go in understanding the criminals in your efforts to be an effective police officer has always been a delicate matter of balance. From the journal of William Miles, Superintendent of Police in Sydney in the 1840s*, it is evident that he went further than most in documenting the criminal milieu and in the

---

* William Augustus Miles was Superintendent of Police in Sydney in the 1840s. Miles kept a notebook in which he compiled details about persons of interest to the police. The *Registry of Flash Men* is a valuable historical document and is now online in the Digital Gallery at www.records.nsw.gov.au.

process developed a sense of familiarity with it. Can we tell from the evidence of the language that he uses whether he crossed the line or not? I think we can.

But first I would like to establish Miles as a policeman of his day talking the jargon of his profession. It is hard for us to get the sense of the word *villain* today because we are so familiar with the modern British use of it among the police meaning simply 'a criminal'. But in the 1800s a villain was someone probably of low birth who was innately disposed to commit all kinds of horrible crimes. It is the contemporary use with a huge dash of moral outrage and prejudice.

Riff-raff were people of low class and disreputable character. A *hocus-pocus man* was someone who tricked you by *leger-de-main* or sleight of hand. A *turf man* was someone who made his living on the racetrack. A *strumpet* sounds archaic to us but to Miles, it was a policeman's ordinary word for a prostitute. The expression *on the town* meant getting a living from prostitution, thieving or the like. And *an exquisite around town* was a dandy or fop. A *piece* was current slang in London for a woman regarded as a sexual object – Miles joked about the villain's supposed niece who was his piece. *Insolent* was very much a policeman's term in its basic sense of 'disrespectful of authority'.

Mixed in with this general policeman's jargon that Miles brought with him from London are the specific terms of Sydney administration in the years of convictism – words like *expiree, special, specialship, stockade, iron gang, exemption man, Norfolk expiree*.

But now we come to the borderline between policeman's jargon and underworld slang. This is where Miles looks across the fence and begins to describe the territory in the words that the criminals would use themselves. It is the kind of decision you make when your level of understanding outgrows the general terms available in formal English and you choose jargonistic words because they are more accurate.

The first of these is the term *flash*, 'the cant language used by the family' to quote James Hardy Vaux, our first lexicographer and a three-times-transported convict. If you are a *flash* person, then you are awake to what is going on, you are in the know. You are one of the crims. A *flash cove* is a thief or fence. A *flash case* is a place where 'the family' hang out.

But there is more that Miles observed from the other side. He describes a few men as *bullies and hangers-on*. We might think we know what that means until we consult dictionaries of cant and find that a *bully* is 'a supposed husband to a bawd or whore' and that to *hang it on* with a woman is 'to cohabit or keep company with her without marriage'. *Fancy* refers to 'any article universally admired for its beauty, or which the owner sets particular store by' so 'a woman who is the particular favourite of any man, is termed his fancy woman, and vice versa'. A *swaggerer* was a London term for what Vaux called a *bouncer* – someone who was out 'to bully, threaten, talk loud, or affect great consequence' for the purposes of intimidation.

A *pall*, spelled thus in Miles' day, was a partner in crime. Highwaymen in particular tended to operate in pairs and referred to each other as *palls*. It was the Americans who sanitised the word as far as we are concerned.

To *sell a man* was 'to betray him by giving information against him'. A man who fell victim to any treachery of this kind, was said to have been 'sold like a bullock in Smithfield'. So when Miles remarks that his criminal contact arranges a meeting that is 'a dead sell to the thieves' we can, thanks to Vaux, understand what he means. The only other citation I have found for this use of *sell* is from *Oliver Twist* so it would seem that Dickens shared Miles' interest in the vernacular of the underworld.

The easiest thing to learn in another language is the nouns – the names for people and things. And Miles has mastered these. He has gone a little bit further to use some of the expressions used instead of the words and phrases that would come naturally to someone of his social standing. But he has not mastered the idiom. The language that Vaux records is full of a detail and liveliness that eludes Miles. For example *bender* – an ironic negative that functioned then in much the same way as the emphatic 'not' does today. 'We did well today – bender!' Or the phrase *Oliver is in town!* that brought attention to the fact that the moon was full and there was an opportunity for nefarious night-time activities. This is the core of the flash language.

We get none of this from Miles, which is to his credit. His interest in detailing the criminal world was laudable and makes fascinating reading today. But he stayed on the right side of the fence as befits a gentleman with interests in natural history and statistics. He must have had a good ear for language and a natural curiosity, which gives his journal a value to us in ways that would not have entered his mind when he was writing it.

Is it unpractical to retain impractical?

Where two derived forms exist it is often the case that we invent a distinction between them. It seems that there is a tendency to opt for *unpractical* as an alternative to *impractical*, a move that had the support of Fowler in his day but might not be greeted with universal enthusiasm today. Fowler's basic argument was that we already had so much of a problem distinguishing between *practical* and *practicable*, that a nice clear-cut negative form would be preferable in both cases. As often happens in these cases, the next step is for us all to develop a slight difference in meaning between the two forms, so that we can happily keep both and add to the usage rules for the linguistically hot and bothered. In this case *unpractical* applies to a person – *he is the most unpractical cook I know* and *impractical* applies to inanimate things – *that is the most impractical scheme I have ever heard of*. So what do we make of the ABC news report that described a scheme to ban 4-wheel drives from around schools as 'unpractical'? Will we go with Fowler all the way?

Down the rabbit hole of usage

How many times do we need to make the same mistake for it to become an accepted usage? How many times, for example, do we need to spell *minuscule* as *miniscule* for people to shrug their shoulders and say 'Okay, *miniscule* it is. Or *minuscule*. Either way. Whatever!'?

This problematic spelling is a good example of how this kind of debate proceeds in the community. The first thing to say is that this is an honest error, not a silly or misguided one. There is an English prefix *mini-* meaning small that is influencing our thinking about the word. Fewer and fewer of us have any training in Latin. The word *minus* in English has to do with subtraction rather than diminutiveness.

Compare this with *advocado* for *avocado*, a mistake caused by clumsiness and that lazy half-grasp of reality that leads to confusion. There is never a chance that *advocado* will be accepted in place of *avocado*. There is no reason why we would bother. With *miniscule* we are seriously and legitimately tempted.

Who is 'we' in this discussion? The language community immediately divides over such issues into those who take a deliberate stand and those who go with the flow. The former group is sometimes labelled 'the educated community' but this is inaccurate. There are those in the second group who are just as educated but in a different sphere, with a different kind of education. Their focus is not language.

Neither is the label 'literary' accurate – members of the first group tend to be writers of a functional kind, writers about writers, writers about aspects of knowledge. Creative writers, while concerned with developing an individual style, are often quite surprisingly unconcerned about language niceties. They leave that to their editors.

So I am going to refer to the first group as 'the deliberative ones' and the second group as 'the intuitive ones'. The deliberative ones tend to look to tradition and analysis. What they were taught to be correct weighs heavily with them, as do arguments from etymology. Members of the second group are guided by their present interpretation of meaning and a contemporary analysis of forms, particularly in relation to pronunciation.

Either group can have a win. Battles were fought over *restauranteur* and *miniscule*. But in each of these cases, quite vehemently in the first and not quite so successfully in the second, the deliberative ones have taught the intuitive ones that this must not be so. The proportion of *miniscule* to *minuscule* spellers has dropped slightly in the past decade.

Sometimes there is a complete victory. The dictionary records such distant battles, as in the case of *adder*, which is more correctly *nadder*. Somewhere in the 12th century, the use of *an adder* for the correct use *a nadder* became accepted. In the same way *a napron* became *an apron*. *Avocado* (meaning 'advocate' in Spanish) is itself an erroneous folk etymology for the Native American Nahuatl word for the fruit *ahuacatl* (which means literally 'testicle'). Such accepted errors are now buried in etymologies.

There will be more such changes. As the deliberative ones rail futilely in the corner of the intellectual world they inhabit, the intuitive ones will be out there altering words at whim without a care in the world.

Vulgarity is ok!

Vulgar language – is there more of it or less of it?

By vulgar language I mean specifically the frequent and inappropriate use of taboo words. In the olden days such words never passed the lips of polite society. In those distant times, newspapers and books faced with an unavoidable vulgarity indicated it with the first and last letter sandwiching substitutional asterisks.

The 1970s loosened the constraints on our language as well as on our hair. And the rise of women's liberation meant that women claimed the right to swear just as colourfully and publicly as men.

A lot of the earlier taboos were to do with sex. While no longer as sexually wild and free as we were in the days of making love and not war, we became much more matter-of-fact about it. If parents are still a bit coy about discussing sex with their children, there is now advice available for children of any age to explain its mysteries, whether the question is from a four-year-old who wants to know where they came from, or from a teenage girl who wants to know whether to go on the pill or not.

It's hard to believe that this means that we are in a tabooless society. But it is the conclusion of various judges and magistrates that words like *fuck* are so commonly uttered and so generally accepted that people cannot be punished by this society for mouthing them. Times have changed, and as far as taboos are concerned, the body has given its all.

Even so, there are words today that in the mere utterance make us flinch.

Derogatory terms are the first category that spring to mind. We are now attuned to the hurtfulness of a range of words to do with race, looks, physical or mental disabilities and sexual preferences. While it has been a salutary thing to raise the level of awareness about the power of words to damage others, it is a process that can be taken to extremes.

Political correctness is doing its best to fill the taboo vacuum by heightening our sensitivities to a new range of words deemed not permissible. We are learning to be shocked by such blunt and old-fashioned adjectives as *old, young, tall, short, male, female*. But somehow these new intellectualised taboos lack the visceral power of those related to the primary life happenings of sex and death.

There is even a suggestion that our sense of taboon-ess has become so effete that the word *fat* in relation to a person is likely to cause more social ripples than the label *fuckwit*. That f-word, on the other hand, is now celebrated with its own special dictionary, *The F-word*, written by Jesse Scheidlower and Lewis Black – *fuck* with all its brothers, cousins and nodding acquaintances. Our neural networks must be completely confused.

For myself, I think I have two options with swearing, neither of them very satisfactory. One scenario is that I roam the house swearing freely at the mess made but with the swear words now having as much effect on me and everyone else as expressions like *Oh bother!* and *Lawksamussy!*. What's the point?

The other scenario is that I am driving in the car with my mother and the f-word just pops out in the stress of sudden braking. I am so mortified and embarrassed on my mother's behalf that I get no pleasure from the experience at all.

In the world of taboos I can't bring myself to break them. In the world without taboos the breakage is painless. I can't win.

A long line of wooden spooners

At the time of the year when sporting winners and losers are announced, we ask ourselves where this term *wooden spooner* came from. At least the teams that have earned this title can comfort themselves that it has a long tradition. It is recorded at Cambridge University in the early 19th century, although it could go back further than that. Apparently the student who came last in the Mathematical Tripos was given this award in jest by the rest of the class. Nor was it a private affair. With the tolerant consent of the authorities, the students hung the spoon over the balcony and lowered it over the winner's head as they received their degree from the Vice-Chancellor. The last recipient in 1909 was an oarsman so the spoon, which by this time had grown to be about one and a half metres in length, was inscribed with an epigram in Greek that translates as:

In Honours Mathematical
This is the very last of all
The Wooden Spoons which you see here
O you who see it, shed a tear.

But while the real wooden spoon is no longer to be seen, the metaphorical one lives on in the wrap-up of every sporting calendar.

What's in a word?

Each year when the *Macquarie* Word of the Year is up for discussion I encounter the difficulty of being misunderstood when I talk about a 'word' in relation to compound items like *brain fade* or *heritage media* or *elevator speech*. 'Not one word but two!', the pedants cry. We all talk about looking up a word in the dictionary and yet dictionary headwords can each have a number of discrete words in them, or combine the words into one solid form, or link them with hyphens. The alternative is to talk about 'lexical items' but I have hesitated to do that because it might seem a little off-putting.

The most common way in which modern English creates new lexical items is by taking two or more existing words and stringing them together to make a compound that means something more than the sum of its parts. We know what an elevator is and we know what a speech is, but none of us would know unless it was explained to us what an *elevator speech* might be. We can guess — a new form of rhetoric in which debating contestants cram into a lift. The real meaning – 'a concise presentation of a product, service, etc., as pitched to someone in the short time available to the presenter as they travel together in a lift' – that we would not guess. If we were Germans we would roll all the bits together into a single-word amalgam. In English half a century ago we would have felt obliged to link words with hyphens a great deal more often than we do today to make the connection clear. Not that we have any difficulty in speech or writing in identifying these compounds, hyphenated or not. We learn them as a semantic unit and they present no problem to us.

It is just the term *lexical item* that seems a bit of a mouthful but if 'word' is going to keep producing the expectation of a single word, then perhaps the followers of the Word of the Year should learn to use the linguist's term.

Wordplay

I thought I should check *sung hero* (as opposed to *unsung hero*) to see if it had much currency. It has some, but not enough yet to treat it as a dictionary item rather than an immediately analysable joke. On the way to reaching this conclusion I travelled through some amusing websites that play on the number of these apparently negative formations that should logically demand a positive form. It is a good source of language humour that has produced some items that have shifted in status from being well-established jokes to straight-faced and legitimate dictionary entries. *Uncouth* produced *couth*, which was at first said with a wry smile. *Macquarie* still notes that it is used humorously. The *American Heritage Dictionary* doesn't bother. *Kempt*, the antonym of *unkempt*, is in a similar situation. Other up-and-coming contenders are, I think, *chalant*, *shevelled* and *ruly*. It is disconcerting to think that the jokes of today may be taken in all seriousness tomorrow.

The other form of wordplay that takes time to settle into the language is the backformation. To *emote* may have started out as a somewhat edgy joke but there is a lot of serious emoting going on now. Similarly, *frivol* (from *frivolous*), *peeve* (from *peevish*) and *sleaze* (from *sleazy*) are established items. A new one that may raise an eyebrow is the singular *specie* (pronounced spee-see) derived from *species*, which is interpreted as a plural form. Some have been created in specialist areas of language – *adolesce* (from *adolescent*) and *lase* (from *laser*). Some have been with us for so long that no one fusses any more about whether they are allowable or not – words like *liaise* and *grovel* and *enthuse*. *Sigh* is a backformation that happened in Middle English. Others happen in other varieties of English and cross over to us, as, for example *summate* from American English.

Yet a third source of amusement is to be found in the fossilised words that appear in phrases, words that have long since lost currency in their own right. When people stop to ponder an expression like *the apple of my eye* it seems on today's interpretation ludicrous. But of course 'apple' in this expression goes back to a meaning it had in Old English. The progression went from the fruit to anything round like the fruit, to the round part of one's eye – the pupil. If something was the apple of your eye, it was so close to you that you couldn't see anything else.

Often such phrases are reinterpreted in strange ways. I remember a hymn that had the battering line 'Oh may the transport last!' The transport referred to was a moment of ecstatic religious contemplation. My father tried to make me believe that it was a plea for a better train system.

Youse

Over the years the editors of the *Macquarie Dictionary* have occasionally been taken to task by people who feel we have let the side down by including the word *youse* in the dictionary.

The dictionary's raison d'être is to be a record of the language choices of the community that have fashioned our own particular variety of English. That means that the fundamental criterion for inclusion in the dictionary is established currency of use. It also means that the dictionary should be a complete record, not a bowdlerised one, of all that is good and bad in our language in terms of both style and content.

Having said that, there is scope in the diction-ary not just to record the existence of a word, but to comment on attitudes towards it. So that the most complete descriptive dictionary is in one sense also prescriptive in that it gives a word an approval rating of some kind based on community consensus.

Sometimes this can become complicated when a word is in a state of flux, with one section of the community regarding it as beyond the pale and another group feeling that it doesn't present a problem at all. The curious dynamics of language are such that although in some instances this can lead to rapid change, in other cases the community can remain in this kind of stand-off for generations.

So does *youse* have currency? Undoubtedly in the spoken language. The defence of *youse* is constructed as follows. Since we abandoned the singular *thou* we have felt the need for some way of differentiating between *you* as a singular pronoun and *you* as a plural pronoun. In writing there is more leisure to construct ways around this ambiguity, but in speech instant clarity is required.

The *English Dialect Dictionary* lists *yous* and *yees* as items from Irish English and comments that *yous* travelled to both American and Australian Englishes. Possibly the lowly status of Irish English in Australia in relation to British English ensured that *yous* would be common in colloquial speech but condemned in formal speech and writing.

But it cannot be ignored. A glance at the corpus of Australian writing shows that there are numerous citations for it in the forms *yous*, *youse* and *yez*. These are usually in dialogue or in a spoken narrative, a context that nevertheless needs to be explained by usage notes and labelling in the dictionary.

While it is true that *youse* needs to be dealt with in the complete record of our English, other dictionaries serve different purposes. The educational range is by necessity prescriptive in many ways. First of all, each dictionary presents a much smaller selection of the words of the language. So a great deal of colloquialism is left out in favour of the jargons of particular subjects being studied. There is no need in such a framework to include representations of speech in the written language.

Prescriptivism is not necessarily a dirty word. And descriptivism is not an open-slather approach to lexicography. Both words get bandied around a good deal but as with all such branding, the words themselves, contrary to nature, lose illumination as they gain heat.

Conclusion

One of the things that I always wanted to have, right from the first edition of the dictionary, was feedback from the users of the dictionary. In that first edition we included a small newsletter that gave people guidance on how to present new words, conducted surveys on aspects of the dictionary, gave a bit of history and background, and so on. Then I discovered radio and have diligently talked on air for decades now, always seeking that sense of what the community was thinking about the words they used. And now we have the internet and a dictionary website and an editor's blog, I can access that community so much more easily and swiftly. Feedback is immediate, conversations can be pursued until we all get a satisfactory outcome.

This book is a distillation of those conversations going back over many years. As author I reserve the right to keep the loudest voice and to add reflections on language over and above the specific issues. But I am grateful to those people who love language and who want to use the dictionary as a working tool for making our use of language always the best it can be.

Acknowledgements

I would like to thank the editors of the Macquarie Dictionary, in particular Alison Moore and Victoria Morgan, who have, for the many years that we have worked together, provided information, workshopped ideas, suggested paths to follow and corrected my spelling. Everyone needs an editor and I have a few. Thanks also to my Macmillan publisher, Ingrid Ohlsson, and editor, Libby Turner, and the Macmillan editorial and production team who have done similar good deeds over a shorter timeframe. Thanks to Helen Bateman, my assigned editor who gave the manuscript the first read, and my husband Richard who gave it the final read. Thanks also to Patrick Cook for conjuring up such an agreeable koala who obviously prefers aitch to haitch!